DATE DUE			

Nicolai I. Bukharin

Economics of the Transformation Period

Nicolai I. Bukharin

ECONOMICS OF THE TRANSFORMATION PERIOD

With Lenin's Critical Remarks

BERGMAN PUBLISHERS
A subsidiary of Lyle Stuart, Inc.
New York

Translated from the Russian original
and from the authorized German edition.

© Copyright, 1971, by Bergman
Publishers, Inc., New York

Standard Book Number: 87503-035-1

Library of Congress Catalog Card Number: 68-58420

Printed in the United States of America

PART I

GENERAL THEORY
OF THE
TRANSFORMATION PERIOD

L 1*

MOSCOW 1920

* The numbers with the prefix "L" indicate Lenin's Marginal Remarks (see pp. 212-224).

TABLE OF CONTENTS

	Page
Preface	9
Chapter I. Structure of World Capitalism	11
Chapter II. Economics, State Power, and War	23
Chapter III. Collapse of the Capitalistic System	33
Chapter IV. General Preconditions of the Building of Communism	60
Chapter V. City and Country in the Process of Social Transformation	81
Chapter VI. Productive Powers, Expenses of the Revolution, and Technological Revolution	97
Chapter VII. General Forms of Organization in the Transformation Period	114
Chapter VIII. System of the Administration of Production under the Dictatorship of the Proletariat	122
Chapter IX. Economic Categories of Capitalism in the Transition Period	133
Chapter X. The "Extra-Economic" Compulsion in the Transition Period	148
Chapter XI. The Process of World Revolution and the World System of Communism	162
Footnotes	174

Afterword to the German Edition   202

Chart 1. a) World Economy in the Epoque of Industrial
            Capitalism   204

         b) World Economy in the Epoque of Finance
            Capitalism   204

      2. System of State Capitalism   205

      3. Process of Social Reproduction   206

      4. State Capitalism and the System of Proletarian
         Dictatorship   207

      5. Collapse of the Old System and the Organization
         of the New   208

      6. Relations Within the Capitalist Hierarchy 209

      7. City and Country in the Transformation Period 210

Lenin's Remarks   211

PREFACE

The purpose of the present book is to refute the usual, vulgar, quasi-Marxian misconceptions about the character of that collapse prognosticated by the great creators of scientific communism, as well as about the character of the changing process from capitalist to communist society. Whoever conceived the revolution of the proletariat as a peaceful transition of power from one hand to the other and the revolution within relationships of production as merely a change in the heads of the organizational apparatus, whoever so imagined the classical model of the revolution of the proletariat—will surely turn away in horror from the world tragedy which the human race is suffering at present. He will not be able, in the smoke of the fire, in the thunder of civil war, to perceive the sublime and solemn outlines of the coming social order. He will forever remain the pitiable Philistine, whose mentality is as cowardly as his "politics." He will attribute his own weakness to the revolution and will invent all kinds of definitions for it except the one it has in reality, the revolution of the proletariat.

The hard experience of life has proven how correct Marx was when he declared: "You will have to go through 15, 20, 50 years of civil wars and national struggles, not only to change conditions but also to change yourselves."*

The old society is splitting, in its form of state as well as in its form of production: it is decaying through and through, down to its darkest depths. Never before has such a powerful rupture occurred. But in no other way could

*"Disclosures about the Trial of Communists in Cologne," Marx-Engels, *Complete Works.* (German edition), Berlin, 1969, Vol. 8, p. 412.

9

the revolution of the proletariat have been executed—the proletariat, which out of the decayed elements is building the foundation of the new society, in a new connection, in new combinations, and according to new principles. And it

L 3 builds as class subject, as organized power, which possesses a plan and the highest will to realize this plan, disregarding all obstacles. Humanity is paying a terrible price for the

L 4 vices of the capitalist system. And only a class such as the

L 5 proletariat, the Prometheus class, will be able to withstand the unavoidable torments of the transformation period and after that, to ignite the torch of communist society.

In the present work I try to present an analysis of the main features of the epoch of transformation. Later, as a second part, I would like to publish a concrete, descriptive work on Russian economy today. The need for such a generalizing work is enormous. A great quantity of material has piled up; it needs to be examined and theoretically developed.

The author's password was: Think through to the end, without shrinking from any consequences. Unfortunately, time was not sufficient to present this work in popular form; thus it had to be written almost in algebraical formulas. The author would consider his work fulfilled if those who have begun an analogous train of thought would put it into a final form, and if those who are holding fast to naive illusions of a reformist nature would at least consider that the thing is much more complicated than it looks in the vulgar pamphlets of the renegades.

L 6 It is superfluous to remark that the author's guideline was the Marxian method—the value of which for the theory of knowledge has by this time been recognized in its entire gigantic greatness.

N. Bukharin

CHAPTER ONE

STRUCTURE OF WORLD CAPITALISM

1. Modern Capitalism as World Capitalism. 2. Subjects of the Economy—State-Capitalist Trusts. 3. Anarchy of World Production and Competition. 4. Crises and Wars. 5. Centralization of Capital.

Theoretical political economy is the science of social economy, which is based on commodity production, i.e. the science of *unorganized* social economy. Only in a society where production is anarchical, just as the distribution of products is anarchical, does the legitimacy of social life reveal itself in the form of "elementary natural laws" which are independent from the will of individuals or of communities, laws which operate with the same "blind" necessity as the "law of gravity . . . when a house falls about our ears."[1] Marx was the first to emphasize this specific character of commodity production, and he has given in his essay on the fetishism of commodities a brilliant sociological introduction into the theory of economics, by establishing it as a *historically limited* branch of science.[2] In fact, as soon as we look at an organized social economy, all fundamental "problems" of political economy, problems of value, of price, of profit, etc. vanish. Here "relations between men" are not expressed as "relations between objects," and social economy is not regulated by blind forces of the market and

11

of competition but by a consciously executed *plan*. Therefore, there is room for a certain system of description on the one side and a system of norms on the other. But there remains no room for a science which studies the "blind laws" of the market, since the market itself is missing. In this way, the end of society based on commodity production also means the end of political economy.

L 8

Thus political economy investigates the economy of *commodities.*

L 9

But the commodity-producing society is in no way congruent with a simple addition of individual economies. Rodbertus in his polemic against Bastiat has already brilliantly explained the presence of a distinct economic milieu or a special connection which he labelled "economic community." If we were dealing with a simple summation of economies, there would be no society. The "sum" is a purely logical unit but not a complex which really exists.

For pure theory it is completely irrelevant how large the extent of the territorial space of the given social economy is. Precisely for this reason Marx ridiculed the term "national economy" which was highly favored by the patriotic German professors. Just as relatively unimportant for abstract theory is the question: who emerges as subject of the single economy? For the present, the *model* of the connection between these economies and particularly the model of the *unorganized connection through exchange* is what is important. However, for a concrete examination which does not limit itself to the derivation of general laws, all these questions are of great importance.

L 10

Modern capitalism is world capitalism. This means that capitalist relations of production dominate in the entire world and that they connect all parts of our planet with one strong, economic bond. In our time, social economy

L 11

finds its concrete expression in world economy. World economy is a *really* existing unit. Therefore, definitions such as the one given by one of the newest scholars, Dr. Karl Tyszka, are completely wrong. Tyszka[3] writes: "Just as the national economy is compounded of the sum of the different types of economies, regardless of whether these are individual economies or corporation economies, so *world economy consists of a sum of national economies.*" "The sum of these national economies, which are substantially influenced by the form of the world market situation, constitutes the world economy." The first definition does not agree with the second; the second conceals an inner contradiction since the concept of a simple summation excludes the organic connection. The sum of crabs in a basket is not a real unit. The number of children born in a year who are "collected" into a statistical total, also represents no real unit. It is only the presence of a special organic *connection* that can make of the simple sum-total a real totality. But just such a totality excludes the concept of an arithmetic sum because it is much larger and more complicated than that sum.

Insofar as the society is one which does not produce products but commodities, it is an *unorganized* unity. The social character of labor and the social character of the production process are here expressed in a constant movement of *exchanged* commodities, in fluctuations of market prices. This social character of labor, however, reveals itself not as clearly and simply as in the case where we have an expedient, social *organization* of labor before us.

Commodity society is a system with a particular *model* of connection, from the character of which emerge the very specific categories of the commodity world. This system is no "teleological unity," i.e. not a consciously *directed* sys-

13

tem according to a determinate plan. Such a plan does not exist. Even the *subject* of the economic process is missing here. Actually, here it is not the "society which produces" but rather "production which takes place within the society." And precisely for that reason man is not master of the product, but the product is master of man, and the "elementary force" of economic development does not fit into the desired frame. If the *total* society in commodity production—therefore also in the capitalist mode of production—is blind, if in its totality it is no teleological unit, then it is likewise so in its single parts. The society consists of such parts, which are linked to one another. Economically active subjects are in this commodity society just these parts, while their system is impersonal, blind, and in this sense irrational.

This "irrationality" constitutes also the fundamental prerequisite for the existence of political economy. But this is precisely what is misunderstood by most of the bourgeois economists. Thus, according to Bernhard Harms,[4] no world economy would exist if there were no international trade agreements. Kobatsch[5] even thinks that there is not yet a world economy at all, that it will not appear until a world state exists. Calwer speaks of the "world market economy." In the entire polemic between Harms and C. Diehl[6] one finds not even a trace of the correct formulation of the question. The search for "regulating" as an essential sign of the economy derives, in fact, from an absolutely false assumption about the nature of the capitalist social organism. To justify a science, one looks for a principle which would signify the death of this science.

Now the question arises, what are the consciously operating component parts of capitalist world economy? Theoretically, world capitalism is conceivable as a system of

14

individual private enterprises. Yet the structure of modern capitalism is such that collective capitalist organizations appear as subjects of the economy: "state-capitalist trusts."[7] | L 12

Finance capital has abrogated the anarchy of production | L 13
within the large capitalist countries. The monopolistic associations of producers, the combined enterprises, and the penetrating of bank capital into industry have created a new type of production relations, by transforming the unorganized system of commodity capitalism into an *organization* of finance capitalism. In place of the unorganized relationship between one enterprise and the others through buying and selling, an organized relationship has to a great extent come about through "control packages" of stocks, through "participation" and "financing"—all of which find their personal expression in the mutual "managers" of banks and industry as well as in the "concerns" and trusts. In this way the exchange relation, which expresses both *social* division of labor and the split of the socially-producing organization into independent capitalist "enterprises," is replaced by *technological* division of labor within the organized "national economy." The splintering of capitalist production, its anarchic condition, reaches however far beyond the borders of social division of labor. By division of labor one always meant the division of total labor into different "jobs."[8] Specifically, by social division of labor one meant and still means distribution of labor among | L 14
individual enterprises. Capitalist enterprises, which are "independent" from each other, must nevertheless rely on each other because one branch of production supplies raw materials, parts, etc. for the other.

However, one should not confuse two things: the splintering of social labor which *results* from the fact of social

15

division of labor—on the one hand, and the splintering of social labor which negates this division of labor—on the other hand. In fact, individual producers of commodities exist not only because there are different forms of labor. Within the realm of every individual *branch* of production, even within specialized and smaller sectors of production, there exists at the same time a great number of independent producers of commodities. In other words, the anarchic structure of the commodity-producing society finds its expression in the existence of separate "enterprises." These "enterprises" have different relationships to each other: they are either related through buying and selling (heterogeneous enterprises), or they stand vis-à-vis each other as competitors (analogous enterprises). The owner of a tailor shop is related to the clothier because he buys cloth from him, but in reference to another similar producer, he is a competitor, since they are not related by any operations of exchange. The simultaneous existence of a tailoring and a clothing *enterprise* constitutes the expression of social division of labor. On the other hand, the simultaneous existence of a number of tailor enterprises expresses no sort of social division of labor.

This difference must be seriously taken into consideration.

Usually one relates the anarchy of capitalist production to market competition and to nothing else. But now we see that market competition expresses only *one* part, only the one model of the "being" of individual commodity producers, namely, the model of interchanging relationships, which is in no way connected to the division of social labor.

Nevertheless, due to the mutual dependency of *all* parts of the social economy, the *heterogeneous* enterprises also engage in a fight with each other. Capitalist society is a surplus value-producing society. Again, the distribution process is the process of *distribution of surplus value* among the subjects of capitalist economy. In no way does each enterprise realize the surplus value which it *by itself* produces. Even the most elementary law of capitalism—the tendency of the rate of profit towards equalization—absolutely "distorts" such a simplicity of relationships.[9] The picture becomes still more complicated with the creation of all sorts of capitalist monopolies. The result is that the fight over the division of surplus value must take on a different character among the different, economically active subjects (whether individual owners or corporations is, of course, unimportant here). We therefore have to distinguish between three forms of competition:

(1) By *horizontal competition* we mean competition between analogous enterprises. Here the anarchy which appears in the competition does not rest on social division of labor.

(2) By *vertical competition* we mean the fight among heterogeneous enterprises whose separate existence expresses the fact of social division of labor.

L 15

(3) By *combined (compounded) competition* we understand finally the fight between the combined enterprises, i.e. those capitalist units encompassing different branches of production, which therefore transform *social* division of labor into a *technological* division.

As a criterion for subdividing the different forms of competition, the model of the enterprise serves here, which relies, for its part, upon one or another relationship to the social division of labor, i.e. to the fundamental relations of production within the world of commodities.

From this circumscription arises the limitation of the methods of competition. It is actually very clear that while

17

horizontal competition can operate through cheap market prices (the "classical" form of competition), this method must make way for other methods when it comes to vertical competition. And we also really see that capital starts to use as its major role methods of direct pressure, of a certain *action directe*—first of all, the *boycott* as the most elementary form.

New methods of competition stand out even more sharply when the fight leaves the sphere of market relations, even though the fight may have started from these relations. *Price* is the *general* category of the commodity-producing society, and therefore *every* disturbance of the equilibrium finds its expression in a certain movement of prices. The category of *profit* is unthinkable without the category of price. In short, every economic phenomenon in the capitalist world is tied to price in one form or another and therefore also tied to the market. But this does not mean that every economic phenomenon is also a phenomenon of the market. An analogous statement is valid for competition. Up to now we mainly considered *market competition,* which was characteristic for the model of *horizontal* competition in general. But competition, i.e. the battle between capitalist enterprises, can also be fought outside of the market in the actual sense of the word—for example, the fight over spheres of investment of capital, i.e. over the possibility of the expansion of the production process itself. In this case it is again evident that other methods of struggle must be applied here than in the "classical" case of horizontal competition in the market.

We must now return to modern world capitalism.

We already emphasized that the units which constitute the system of modern world economy are not simple enterprises but complicated complexes, "state-capitalist trusts."

Certainly, international tie-ups exist also between single enterprises in different "countries," whereby such relations may be directly opposed in each concrete case, as the "countries" themselves may be. But lately the relations between whole complexes are becoming predominant. Capitalist "national economy" has moved from an *irrational system* to a *rational organization,* from a subject-less economy to an economically active subject. This transformation has been effected by the growth of finance capitalism and the fusion of the economic and political organization of the bourgeoisie. At the same time, however, neither the anarchy of capitalist production in general nor the competition of capitalist commodity producers was eliminated. These phenomena have not only remained but have deepened by reproducing themselves in the framework of *world* economy. The system of world economy is just as blindly irrational and "subject-less" as the earlier system of *national* economy.

L 15 a

Commodity economy by no means completely disappears, although it either dies out or shrinks within a nation by making room for organized distribution. The commodity market actually becomes only a *world* market and ceases being "national." Here the identical process is observed as in the merging of two or more heterogeneous enterprises to a combined unit, where the raw materials are transformed to a semi-finished product and then to the end-product— but so that the corresponding movement of products is not accompanied by an opposite movement of money equivalents; the "economic goods" *within* the combined enterprises are put into circulation not as commodities but as products, and they represent commodities only insofar as they are hurled out of the combined total complex. In the same way, the product whose distribution is organized

19

within the nation, is only a commodity insofar as its being is connected with the existence of the world market. The difference—compared to the national economy—lies mainly in the extent of the national economic system and in the character of the components of this system.

The particular character of state-capitalist trusts explains to us also the particular model of competition. The state-capitalist trust is actually a gigantic combined enterprise. State-capitalist trusts vis-à-vis each other oppose each other not only as units which produce one and the same "world commodity" but also as parts of the social division of world labor, as units which *complement* each other economically. Therefore the struggle of competition goes on simultaneously in a *horizontal* as well as in a *vertical* line; this struggle is *compounded competition.*

The transition to the system of finance capitalism increasingly intensified the transformation process from simple horizontal market competition to combined competition. Since the method of the fight corresponds to the model of competition, there followed inevitably a "critical development of relationships" on the world market. Vertical and combined competition are accompanied by *methods of direct power influence.* Therefore the system of world finance capital unavoidably brings about the *armed conflict* of imperialist competitors. *Here lies also the root of imperialism.*

L 16

The struggle of the finance-capitalist state organizations is the crassest expression of the contradictions and the anarchy of the method of capitalist production, where labor socialized on a world scale comes into conflict with the state-"national" subjects of appropriation. The conflict between the development of productive forces and capital-

20

ist production relations must—insofar as the whole system does not explode—temporarily *reduce* the productive forces so that another cycle of their development under the same capitalist veil can begin. Such destruction of productive forces constitutes the *conditio sine qua non* of capitalist development, and from this point of view the crises constitute the costs of competition and—as a special case of these costs—wars create the necessary *faux frais* of capitalist reproduction. A transitory equilibrium is actually achieved here in two ways: first, through direct decrease of the productive forces, which finds its expression in a *destruction of values;* second, by partial elimination of frictions between the individual elements of the economic system. The second way expresses itself in the *centralization of capital.*

Centralization of capital consumes competition but on the other hand reproduces it on an extended base. Centralization destroys the anarchy of *small* units of production, but it thereafter aggravates the anarchic relationships between the *large* sectors of production. "Frictions" in the economic system as a whole disappear in one place, only to emerge in another place in much greater dimensions; they transform themselves into frictions between the basic sectors of the great *world* mechanism.

Centralization of capital takes place according to the same three basic rules by which competition proceeds: it is either *horizontal* centralization, if analogous enterprises are absorbed, or *vertical* centralization if heterogeneous enterprises are amalgamated, or finally, *combined* centralization, if a combination of combinations or a combination from a combined and a simple enterprise occurs. In *world* economy, centralization of capital finds its expression in

21

imperialist annexations, which can be differentiated in exactly the same way according to the three basic rules of competition.[10]

L 17

We perceive as a result of wars the same phenomena as result from economic crisis; next to the disturbance of productive forces we find the annihilation of small and medium-sized world groupings (decline of independent states) and the formation of still greater combinations, which grow at the cost of the declining groups.

L 18

Production relations in the capitalist world do not limit themselves to the relation between the "producers of commodities," i.e. to the relation between single capitalists and their organizations (syndicates, trusts, nations). Modern world economy is not only a commodity economy but also a *capitalist* commodity economy. And the contradictions between the individual sectors of this economy are found at *two* main levels: at the level of anarchic correlation between the enterprises, and at the level of the anarchic construction of society as *class* society. In other words: there exist "pure economic" contradictions as well as "social" contradictions. It is evident that the first category of relationships exerts a direct influence upon the second. The destruction of the productive forces and the process of capitalist centralization critically sharpen the contradictions between the classes, and upon a certain combination of both these factors, a *collapse of the whole system* takes place, which begins with the organically weakest links of this system. That is precisely the beginning of the communist revolution.

CHAPTER TWO
ECONOMICS, STATE POWER, AND WAR

1. War and the State.   2. Theory of the State.   3. Economics, State Power, and War in their Interchanging Relation.   4. Classification of Wars. Imperialist Wars. Socialist Wars.   5. Class War and Civil War.

The War of 1914-18 has categorically raised the question of state power. When before the war, even in the Marxist camp, points of view clothed in fairly thick Manchester colors were disseminated, so we see from the moment that the imperialist state threw millions and more millions of people into the whirlpool of history and in one stroke revealed its colossal significance as an *economic* factor—from that moment on, the analysis of state power has been included in the agenda of theoretical and practical discussions.

The life of the all-absorbing state organization—not the life of the society but that of the state—moved to the fore. If old Hobbes in his *Leviathan* wrote[11] that there was no power which could be compared with the power of the state, then his *Leviathan* is really nothing compared with that powerful force revealed by the state apparatus of finance capital.

In class society war is waged by the state organization. In capitalist society the contradictory economic structure

23

of society finally leads to a sharp crisis of its political formation. This happens in two main directions: the anarchy of world capitalism—the opposition between social world labor and "national"-state appropriation—expresses itself in the collision of state organizations of capital and in capitalist *wars;* on the other side, the opposition between the classes of capitalist society, which opposition is enormously sharpened by the development of the first opposition, leads to *revolution.* Here as well as there, the question of the given state organization is decisive. The *war* calls forth a regrouping of the forces upon the same base: the model of state power and its social content remain. The *revolution* also changes the basis of the state organization by bringing a new class to the helm and by calling a new model of the state to life.

The questions about war and state power are therefore the most acute of our epoch and demand to be solved. Here we want to broach them above all purely theoretically.

Marxism considers all social phenomena in their connections and interchanging relationships; each series of these phenomena thereby forms one link in the chain of causes, through which a particular model of production relations, a particular "economic structure" of society, is either preserved, developed, or, on the contrary, destroyed. One must also consider war and state power from this point of view.[12]

Every class society is a mechanism producing surplus product which is put at the disposal of a part of this society. This surplus product can assume the form of value (for instance, in capitalist economy), or remain simply product (slave economy). In the one case as in the other, however, we have before us a process of exploitation. Now let us ask the question quite generally: How is this process of exploitation possible? How can a system exist which harbors such

24

violent internal contradictions? How is it that society, which basically consists of *two* societies (classes), can exhibit a relative unity? In other words: by what is the preservation of the relative social equilibrium, of the stability of the social system which rests on a split of the social whole, made possible?

The answer is clear. When such a system exists, something must also exist which serves as a supplementing factor, which *holds* the split society *together* and suppresses (in the "rough" physical and "fine" ideological sense) the resistance of the oppressed classes. In short, to preserve this system, an organization is necessary which rules not only the things but mainly also the *people*. Such an organization is the *state*.

However, it should not be supposed that the state were a thing which stands *above* the society and *above* the classes. The society contains no elements of any kind which stand above the classes. On the other hand, the basic function of the state exists, as we have already seen, in the preservation, fortification, and extension of the process of exploitation in as much as there is rule by the minority. From this it follows that the state organization can be *only and solely* an organization of the ruling class, or as Engels already wrote[13]: ". . . the state is an organization of the possessing class for its protection against the non-possessing one."

L 19

This condition must be especially emphasized. In fact, the relative possibility of existence of the entire socially contradictory system could, taken theoretically, be reached in two ways: either through the existence of a "third power," which reconciles the classes, smoothes over the oppositions, and promotes a permanent form of compromise, or on the other hand through the existence of an organization of the one camp which uses all means at its disposal—from direct application of violence to the most complicated ideological structure—to keep in check the camp of its class enemies. In reality we must deal with the second solution to the question, i.e. with the existence of an organization of the ruling classes. But most theoretical constructions, even the quasi-Marxist ones, emphasize the first, "harmonic" theory of state power.

Actually, this "theoretical" wisdom could already be found in the codex of the Babylonian king Hammurabi, namely, the goal of the ruler is the securing of the law of the land, the elimination of the Evil and the Bad, so that the Strong will not hurt the Weak.[14] The "most weighty" of arguments in favor of this honorable "theory" is that of the existence of so-called functions of state power conducive to the public good: the construction of railroads and hospitals, the enacting of laws governing factories, insurance, etc.

Upon an unprejudiced examination, however, it turns out that these functions of state power in no way exclude its pure class character. Either they constitute the necessary condition for extension of the process of exploitation itself (railroads), or they take care of other interests of the ruling classes (sanitary measures), or they are strategic concessions to the class enemy.[15]

The same thing occurs here as in every organization *whatsoever* of the ruling class. A trust or syndicate has the goal of increasing profit but not of nourishing the people or providing work. For the purpose of profit increase, however, it must direct production and employ workers, whom it grants concessions in certain cases (strikes) without ceasing for a moment to be a businessman's or as the German workers say, "Scharfmacher" organization. The functions "conducive to the public good" are here none other than a *necessary condition of exploitation*.

26

From the standpoint of the objective role as well as from the standpoint of the subjective-collective goal that the state sets for itself as the organization of people who "make their own history," the social function of this state (and therefore also its "essence") exists in the protection, the fortification, and the development of those *relations of production* which correspond to the interests of the ruling classes.

The chief characteristic of the state organization of the ruling class, whereby this organization is distinguished from other organizations of the same class, is its universality. The state organization is the most far-reaching organization of the class, in which it concentrates its entire strength, in which the tools of mechanical pressure and of repressive measures[16] are concentrated, in which the ruling class is organized specifically as *class* and not as a small part or small group of a class. Thus it happens that every "economic" action, in as far as it comprehends an entire class, inevitably assumes a "political" character: here the blows are directed not against an individual group but against the class as a whole and consequently against its state power.

L 20

The state is a specific human organization. It is in this way the expression not of the technical relationships of man to nature but of the *social* relationships of men among each other, of man to man. It would be entirely wrong to seek the "essence" of the state in its technical-organizational definitions, for instance, that it represents a centralized apparatus. For the abstract concept of centralization can presuppose diametrically-opposed models of social relationships, and in the very latter model lies the essence of the matter. "A Negro is a Negro, and man of the black race. But only under specific relations does he become a slave."

27

The means of production are always means of production. That is a technical concept. But only under specific relationships do these means of production become capital: and to be sure, only when a specific social interchanging relation in them begins to be reified, a relationship of a very special quality which actually constitutes the "essence" of capital. "Capital is not a thing but a social relationship." (Marx)

To Marx all social phenomena are historical, and in the historical specificity Marx seeks their constitutive marks. Therefore it is not surprising that the state, from the standpoint of Marxism, represents a thoroughly historical category, and in fact a category of class society. But that which is "essential" in the state is not the fact that it is a centralized apparatus but that this centralized apparatus embodies in itself a specific relationship between the classes, namely the relationship of domination, of power, of oppression and enslavement. It is the apparatus which *will disappear,* together with the disappearance of the classes and of the final form of class domination, the dictatorship of the proletariat.[17]

L 21

Of the bourgeois investigators, Ludwig Gumplowicz and Franz Oppenheimer, who were strongly influenced by Dühring, are the closest to the truth. Oppenheimer defines the "historical state" in the following way:

"In its *form,*" he writes, "it (the state) is an institution of law imposed by a victorious group upon a subjugated group. Its content is the managing of the undergroup by the overgroup."[18] Without going into the question of the conquest and the origin of classes themselves exclusively from the fact of "extra-economic" pressure,[19] we must recognize Oppenheimer's formulation of the "managing" as in essence correct (which does not prevent this author in his

28

other works from overflowing with sympathy for the "class-less" Prussian bureaucracy and complimenting it).

From the above analysis of state power we can clearly see its character as a "superstructure" upon the economic base. Like every "superstructure," this one too is not simply a glass shade covering the economic life but an active power, an operating organization, which secures on all sides the base of production upon which it arose.

Now we must raise another question, the question of *war*. This question too we must grasp from the same standpoint from which we approached the question of state power. What place does war have in the stream of social life? And since social life is above all a process of reproduction and succession of social relationships of production—what role does war, especially, play in this?

It is no longer difficult to answer this question. War is not waged by "peoples" nor by "nations": it is waged by *states*, which utilize the living strength of the "people" on the slaughter fields in exactly the same way they utilize them in the factories or in the mines. The *army*—that tool which is set into motion as soon as war begins—is the most essential component of the state apparatus. Here we want to mention incidentally that the entire social structure is characterized by a peculiar monism of its architecture: all its parts have one and the same "style." Just as in production relationships men are arranged according to a specific hierarchical scale, corresponding to class groupings, so in the state apparatus itself and in the army particularly this social hierarchy is reflected.

However, when on the one hand war is a function of the state, the state power *in actu*, and when on the other hand the state as an apparatus is a means for fortifying and extending specific production relations, then it is evident that

L 22

29

war also performs this "work" above all. The fight between specific bases of production which are personified in the ruling class of the states expresses itself in the fight between states. Every production structure has an adequate model of state power and consequently also an *adequate model of war.* Here we are not interested in the technological-organizational side of the essence of war (although that too is determined by the general technological and economic relationships). We are here interested in the social meaning of this phenomenon. In order to answer the question about the "essence" of war, we must tackle this question just as historically as the question of the state. Then we will get a similar answer, namely, that war from the sociological standpoint is a *means for the reproduction of those production relationships on the basis of which it arises.*

L 23

The state is an "extra-economic factor." Nevertheless, it has powerful economic significance. In the same way, war as a function of state power, while being an "extra-economic" factor, constitutes one of the most powerful levers of the economic process.[20]

The problem must be detailed in further theoretical analysis, for the social process is not only the extension of a specific production structure. It is also the process of *replacing* one form, one "way of production," one "economic structure" by another. But the replacement of the "bases" is also accompanied by the necessary changing of the façade of the state. The new production relations burst open the old political shell.

Every phase of historical development and every model of production relations, however, has its specific legitimacy. In order to understand any epoch theoretically, one must consider it in its very peculiarities and analyze each of its characteristics which make this epoch expressly an epoch, i.e. which create a particular model of relationships, and above all of production relationships. Still, when we now uncover the laws of social development on the basis of this method, it is clear that, as a consequence of the relatedness of all phenomena of public life, we must also examine wars in the same way.

Through that which has been said, we have laid the basis for a *classification* of wars. It is the same basis as for the classification of states. Every production model also has a corresponding model of state, and for every model of the state there corresponds a quite specific model of war. | L 24

Let us cite some examples. We have, for example, an economy based on slavery. The state is nothing other than a slaveholding state, and the war of this state is nothing other than a means of extending this slave regime, of extending the reproduction of the production relations of the slaveholding society. The so-called colonial wars of Spain, Holland, France, etc. were wars of capitalist trade states. Their social role aimed at an extension of the relations of capitalist trade production, which later were transformed into relations of industrial capitalism. As industrial capital and its state organizations entered the struggle for markets, wars began to subject the "backward" world to the rule of industrial capital. Finally, as the capitalist method of production enveloped itself in the form of finance capitalism, there emerged immediately a particular model of state power, the rapacious, imperialist state with its centralized military apparatus, and the social role of war consisted from then on of the extension of the sphere of domination of finance capital with its trust and bank consortia. | L 25

It is just the same when war is waged by a socialist, dictatorial government. The workers' state which wages war is concerned with extending and fortifying that economic base upon which it arose, namely socialist production relations. (From this follows, among other things, the admissibility in principle of revolutionary, socialist wars of aggression.) A totally new model of state power corresponds to production which becomes socialist. This model of state power is distinguished from all earlier ones, insofar as socialist methods of production are distinguished from all previous methods of production, which were based on the economic relations of private property. Therefore, the social meaning of war waged by the workers' dictatorship is by principle different from all wars of previous epochs without exception.

L 26 Socialist war is *class war*, which must be distinguished from simple *civil war*. The latter is not war in the true sense of the word, for it is not war between two *state* organizations. In class war, on the other hand, *both* sides are organized as state powers—on the one side the state of finance capital, on the other side the state of the proletariat.

We have considered all phenomena in their pure form. In reality the matter is of course much more complicated. Modern world economy, in spite of the powerful centralization of capital, represents nevertheless a fairly colorful picture. And even the world war exhibited, next to the purely imperialist elements, a series of other elements which were sprinkled into the keynote. For example, the national chauvinism of the small nations, which now—for one historical moment—become independent bourgeois state units. But the fate of the world will not be determined by, if one may say so, this petit bourgeoisie of states; it will be determined by the mutual relation between the colossi of imperialism, and in the last analysis the struggle between the colossi of class war will be the decisive one.

CHAPTER THREE
COLLAPSE OF THE CAPITALIST SYSTEM

1. War and the Organization of Capitalist Production Relations (State Capitalism). 2. The Reproduction Process, the Productive Powers, and War. 3. The Monistic Construction of Capitalist Society and its Anarchy. 4. The Collapse of Capitalist Society. 5. Communism as the Only Way Out. Its Historical Necessity. 6. Productive Powers and the Expenses of the Revolution.

The clash of different parts of the world capitalist system, in which was expressed the conflict between the growth of the powers of production of this system and its anarchical structure of production, was, as we have seen, a conflict of state capitalist trusts. The objective need which history placed on the agenda is the need for an organization of world economy, i.e. for the transformation of the *subject-less* world economic system into an economically active *subject*, into an expediently operating organization, into a "teleological unity," into an *organized* system. Imperialism attempts to solve this task by its own methods. This is formulated, not entirely correctly, by H. von Beckerath. "Since free competition," he says, "fails as regulator of economic life, the call for organization finally resounds.

33

People unite and wage war in common for industrial market territories. Thus arises a struggle of nationally united economic masses with increasingly stronger political emphasis. It finally culminates in a giant political struggle of the nations fighting for the industrial export outlets."[21] The mastering of this task surpassed the power of imperialism, and the war crises led to a crisis of the whole system. But in the *narrow* frame of individual state capitalist trusts, the first stage of the war was a stage of internal *reorganization* of capitalist relations of production in terms of the planning and organization of the *partial systems* which are fighting with each other. It is not difficult to understand and follow the basic causes of this reorganization which led to the abolishment of the internal anarchy of production on the way to the nationalization of economic functions. *Organizationally and technologically* this reorganization was highly facilitated by the process of the exceptionally quick dying out of the middle groups. War in this respect had the effect of a gigantic crisis. While the sum of the produced surplus value decreased, it was concentrated and accumulated in the (socially, technologically, and economically) strongest production units. The process of *centralization* of capital was exceptionally accelerated, and this accelerated centralization formed the "negative condition" of the new form of capitalist relationships. The *positive cause* of nationalization was constituted by the *needs of war* as a powerful, organized process. The extent of war, its technology, the complicated internal relations of the military apparatus, the enormous demand for industrial and agricultural products, which set in immediately on the part of the war organization, and finally for the ruling classes the importance of the end of war operations placed on the agenda the greatest possible overcoming of anarchy within

34

the fighting capitalist partial systems. All conditions being equal, the war results were directly proportional to the degree of economic organization of the state capitalist trusts. The causes mentioned were exceptionally sharpened by the *lack of many products,* especially of raw materials, a lack which appeared immediately following the break in international relations and kept increasing with the general exhaustion and impoverishment.[21a] This lack understandably required the most frugal and, consequently, rationalized, organized distribution possible. But since the process of distribution is one of the phases of the process of reproduction, it is obvious that the organizing of distribution had to lead just as inevitably to a greater or lesser organizing of the production process. It is easy to understand that the class of capitalists in its totality (and dynamically they are the representatives of finance capital) profited exceptionally by this centralization. Only completely naive persons saw in this a violation of the law of sacred private property. In reality, there was not a trace of any "expropriation of the expropriators," for everything centralized itself in the hands of the *finance capitalist* state organization and not in the hands of some "third" power. Opposition came mainly from circles of *backward* strata of the bourgeoisie, above all from representatives of commercial capital and commercial speculation. The organization of production and distribution essentially excludes commerce in general and commercial speculation in particular; therefore it excludes commercial profit and "differential profit,"[22] profit from speculation. As far as this organization of production and distribution is actually carried out, it breaks the "sacred laws" of especially these categories. Still it would be ridiculous to assume that therefore the "laws" of the capitalist class as a whole are transgressed. Here there occurs merely a new distribution of surplus value in favor of finance capitalist groups, a transformation of commercial profit into dividends or interest, which is paid out by the state bank. Consequently, surplus value is not eliminated, but rather the *form* of a part of this surplus value merely changes. And it is here that the essence of state capitalist organization exists in as much as it is concerned with categories of profit and of distribution of surplus value. As far as the diminution of a certain part of surplus value and its transferral to the workers as security against the revolution is concerned, that is a secondary consideration which plays no essential role.[23] The mathematical limit of this tendency is given by the transformation of the entire "national economy" into an absolutely closed *combined trust,* where all excess "enterprises" have ceased to be enterprises and have transformed themselves into mere individual workshops, into *branches* of this trust, where therefore the *social* division of labor has transformed itself into a *technical* division of labor and where the entire economy has become an absolutely unified enterprise of *corresponding groups of world bourgeoisie.*

The common principle of organization of this form of capitalism was the subordination of all economic (and not only economic) organizations of the bourgeoisie to their *state.* For understandable reasons. In fact, let us take a whole series of bourgeois organizations: the state, the syndicates, the cartels and trusts, employer associations, corporations, bank consortia, research institutes, organized bourgeois journalism, and hundreds more. Theoretically considered, it is perfectly clear that this whole system will have reached a maximum stability through a union, a cohesiveness, a coordination of all these organizations. But which organization is to be at the top? It is again clear:

the greatest, the most powerful, the most comprehensive. Such an organization is state power. The state organization of the bourgeoisie concentrates within itself the entire power of this class. Consequently, all remaining organizations—above all the economic and then also the others—must be subordinated to the state. All are "militarized." They are all transformed into branches, into divisions of the unified, the *universal* organization. Only under these conditions does the entire system preserve maximum stability. Thus there arises a new model of state power, the classical model of the *imperialist* state, which relies on *state capitalist* relations of production. Here "economics" is organizationally fused with "politics"; the economic power of the bourgeoisie unites itself directly with its political power; the state ceases to be a simple protector of the process of exploitation and becomes a direct, capitalist collective exploiter, openly opposed to the proletariat.[24] The unfolding of state power reveals here its complete dialectical nature. State power arose as the original and unified form of organization of the ruling class. It then became one of the many organizations of the bourgeoisie; and finally it again became an essentially unified organization after it had *absorbed everything else.*[25]

State capitalist relations of production are, logically and historically, a continuation of finance capitalist relations, and constitute the completion of the latter. It is therefore not surprising that the starting point of their development constituted those organizational forms which were given by finance capital, i.e. syndicates, trusts, and banks. In place of trusts as private monopoly organizations, which not only commercially but also technologically encompass production, appears the *state monopoly*. The trust-like syndicates and cartels are likewise replaced by state monop-

37

olies. The process of centralization is accelerated through the pressure of state power: there arise so-called *compulsory syndicates and compulsory cartels. Mixed* enterprises constitute the model of transition where the state enters the scene as co-owner, as large stockholder, etc., and where the form of finance capitalist relatedness between the state and private enterprise expresses itself in the form of the so-called "sharing" ("participation"). These most important forms—in terms of the restructuring of production relations—are by no means the only ones: to them belong also a whole series of less essential changes such as state regulation and control of the production process (forced production, standardization, regulation of methods of production and of the internal technical system of production in general); regulation of distribution (controlled delivery and controlled reception; state provision, state warehouses, price rating, system of ration cards, etc. etc.[26] The banks play a special and thereby exceptionally large, organizational role. They bring investments into the *state bank,* which then centralizes the huge sums (it is sufficient to recall war loans in themselves) and channels them to the war industry. Since the investments represent to a certain degree capital which periodically becomes liquid, so their organizational "distribution" by the state bank signifies the actual subjugation of industry to the state bank and the transformation of industrial profit into interest paid out by this bank. Consequently, capitalist relations of production transform themselves also in this way to state capitalist ones, and different kinds of capitalist profit equalize each other, and are transformed into a peculiar "dividend," which is paid out by a unified, capitalist collective enterprise, a unified stock company, a trust, as represented by the imperialist state.[27]

The models of organizational relatedness in its concrete form are different here; they are distinguished by their functional character: here we are also concerned with a *planned organization,* where new, stable units of techno- logical production originate (compulsory trusts could serve as examples which centralize a whole series of previous production associations, or state monopolies, etc.); there is also simple *"regulation"* (e.g. control of market and in- come); finally there is another minor element of the or- ganizing process—*standardization.*[28] As an example of the latter, sales taxation. But it would be false to overlook the fact that the general tendency of "state capitalist" develop- ment by which the tendency of finance capitalism is accel- erated, moves in the direction of *higher* organizational models, which achieve a stable grouping of *technological production.* The organizational process does not have to begin with the aspect of technological production; the sub- jective goal of its agents can be not the organization but, let us say, the purely *commercial* bookkeeping—and never- theless the objective end result can be the creation of new complexes of technological production. Such a phenom- enon could be perceived in the period of finance capitalism with greatest clarity: syndicates originated as *commercial associations* which operated in the market; but, neverthe- less, further development led to the achievement of trust- like cartels and then to the formation of real trusts, i.e. of associations not only of a commercial nature but also of a production-technological nature. Or another example. The penetration of bank capital into industry led to the consoli- dation of the enterprises ("fusions," combined trusts, etc.). In these cases, processes of organization proceed from the sphere of circulation to the sphere of production; that re- sults because the process of circulation forms a component

39

of the general total process, of the reproduction process, which possesses an inevitability for all its parts and phases.[29]

Therefore: *the reorganization of production relations of finance capital went in the direction of the state capitalist universal organization, with the elimination of the commodity market, with the transformation of money into a counting unit, with production organized on a state-wide scale, with the subordination of the entire "national economic" mechanism to the aims of world competition, i.e. above all to the aims of war.*

In the above analysis we have considered the organizational forms with the help of which the capitalist structure of the individual countries adjusted to the new conditions of existence of world capitalism as a whole. But we considered all changes from the viewpoint of the overcoming of the anarchy of *production*. Now something has to be said about *social* anarchy. The totality of production relations encompasses not only the relationships between the people as they are organized according to *enterprises* alone; there exists also another differentiation of these production relationships in as much as we speak of relationships between *classes*. Consequently, a restructuring of relationships has to occur in this direction too, for otherwise the entire system would be unstable and of short respite. The needs of war also played a powerful part here, because the mobilization of the proletariat and its leaders in the name of war was for the imperialist war leadership a necessary supposition just as was the mobilization of material production.

The process of overcoming the anarchy of production had for its starting point organizational elements already worked out by finance capital. The process of *social* reorganization had to rely just as much upon those factors which had been created by the preceding development. The *material forms of organization* existed in the *workers organizations:* in the trade unions, in the socialist parties, and partly in the co-operatives, with all their auxiliary and secondary apparatus. The *ideological forms* consisted of the peculiar mentality of *workers patriotism,* which partly represented a conversion of the vestiges of the old petit bourgeois mentality but partly represented the product of the relative and temporary interest of the working class in imperialist politics. Finally, the *method* of restructuring was the same method as the *subordination to the all-encompassing bourgeois state.* The betrayal of the socialist parties and the unions expressed itself in the very fact that they entered into the service of the bourgeois state, that they were actually nationalized by this *imperialist* state, that they transformed themselves into labor departments of the military machine. The *nationalization of these organizations* had as ideological equivalent the peculiar *bourgeois nationalization of the proletarian mentality;* this expressed itself in the fact that the theory of the so-called "party truce" achieved wide-spread dissemination and was even recognized by proletarian circles. Of course, along with these methods there developed, as usual, methods of direct mechanical influence and repression, methods of *direct coercive measures.*

In this way, the highest possible stability of parts of the capitalist system was achieved under the conditions created by the great imperialist war, i.e. under the conditions of the terrible loss of equilibrium in the entire *world* system of capitalist society.

So that our examination may touch upon all basic tendencies of the organization of the capitalist system, we must

41

also mention the *syndicates of the state capitalist trusts,* those peculiar "second class" syndicates, which have the state capitalist trusts as their component parts. These include, for instance, the "Coalition of States" or the "League of Nations." The preconditions for these organizations are provided by finance capitalist associations and the total sum of mutual "sharing." The war intensified the process of this loose syndicalization of state capitalist trusts; the inter-allied Labor conferences were, among others, an expression of the same tendency. Here the tendencies towards organization cross the borders of the individual state. Consequently, the process of organization has found its highest expression in these experiments of the capitalist world.

All these processes were completed under conditions of *vast annihilation of productive powers.* The rebuilding of the structure was accompanied by a decline of productive powers. This resulted finally in the inevitable collapse of the entire system. It is our task to examine the basic influences of the process of destruction.

By productive powers of the society we understand *the totality of the means of production and of labor powers.* That means therefore the totality of machines of all kinds, of raw materials, fuel, etc. *in natura* on the one hand, and the totality of labor powers of all kinds *in natura* (the labor powers of metal workers, of technicians, of textile workers, etc., i.e. the labor powers of diverse concrete character and of diverse qualification, on the other hand.)[30] The unfolding of productive powers is the base of human development in general, and from this very point of view must every fact of public life be considered. The point of view of the development of productive powers agrees with the point of view of *reproduction:* the unfolding of productive powers corresponds to expanded reproduction, its stationary condition corresponds to simple reproduction; its sinking finds its expression in the reproducing of an increasingly smaller part of periodically consumed products. In the last case we have a social step backward.

The point of view of *reproduction* is actually compulsory for every economic examination. But it is *twice as compulsory* for the economist who investigates "critical" periods and transitional phases of development. In fact: in so-called "normal" periods, periodic repetition of the cycle of production is given from the outset. Naturally, specific problems arise here, too—especially in capitalist society —but on the whole a more or less "smooth" course of events can be presupposed. "Critical" epochs, however, make each successive production cycle doubtful. Therefore, the point of view of reproduction is, methodologically speaking, the *only* correct point of view here. For it examines the very conditions of *repeatability* of production cycles, i.e. the conditions of the *dynamic* equilibrium of the social system. "Reproduction, taken literally, is simply again-production, repetition, renewal of the process of production, and it may not be apparent at first glance wherein the concept of reproduction is actually distinguished from the generally understandable concept of production and why a new, strange expression should be necessary. But alone in the very repetition, in the constant return of the production process, lies an important moment in itself."[31] That was "actually" already excellently comprehended by the physiocrats, but the "learned," liveried lackeys of imperialism have thoroughly forgotten it. That was the reason that the war in its beginning produced truly enormous theoretical constructions which deduced a "beneficial" (!) influence of war upon "national economic life" from the fact of war

43

profiting, from the "flourishing" of war industry, and from the growth of the stocks of metallurgic, chemical, and other factories.

Let us now consider the *real* reproduction process, insofar as the total economy stands under the influence of war, i.e. insofar as a *re-distribution of productive powers in the interest of the war industry* and the providing for the army has taken place. It is customary to characterize labor transformed for war needs as unproductive labor from an economic point of view. What does this mean? The specific meaning of this labor becomes clear when we examine its influence upon the *conditions of reproduction.* In the "normal" process of production, means of production and means of consumption are created. These are the two most important areas of the entire economy. It is clear that the means of production are in every case embodied in the means of social labor. Their production is a condition for reproduction. It is just so, on the whole, with the production of the means of consumption. These means of consumption in no way disappear without a trace for the continued cycles of the process of production. For the process of consumption is *basically* a particular process of the *production of labor power.* Labor power is, however, just as necessary a condition for the process of reproduction. Consequently, the production of means of consumption as well as the production of means of production delivers products which constitute the necessary condition of the process of reproduction, without which the latter could not take place. War production has a completely different meaning: a cannon does not transform itself into an element of the new cycle of production; powder is shot into the air and in no way appears in a new shell in the following cycle. On the contrary. The economic effect of these elements *in actu* is

44

of purely negative quantity. Still, one should not think that the economic significance is necessarily tied to the particular kind of *use* value and the objective form of the product. Let us observe the *means of consumption* with which the army is supplied. Here we perceive the same thing. The means of consumption do not produce *labor powers,* for the soldiers do not figure in the process of production; they are eliminated from it, they are *outside* of the process of production. As long as the war lasts, so long do the means of consumption serve, therefore, for the large part, not as means of production of *labor power* but as means of production of specific "soldier power," which plays no role in the process of production. As a result, the process of reproduction assumes with the war a "deformed," regressive, *negative* character, namely: with every successive production cycle the real base of production grows narrower and narrower, the "development" is carried out not in a widening but in a continually narrowing spiral.

Here another important circumstance must be emphasized. The army, which provides a powerful demand, i.e. needs to be supported, offers no work equivalent. As a result, it does not produce but rather deprives. In other words: there occurs here a *double* deficit in the "reproduction-stock." This circumstance represents the most important destructive factor. Besides this, the direct destructions of war (destroyed roads, burned cities, etc.) must be taken into consideration, just as a whole series of indirect destructions (of labor power, and others). Thus it is clear that the real base of social production narrows with each circulation of social capital. We are not concerned here with an expanded reproduction, not even with a simple reproduction; we have here a permanently increasing *underproduction*. This process can be designated as *expanded*

negative reproduction. That is war, considered from an economic point of view. The *real* process taking place is therefore an expanded *negative* reproduction. This process must
be distinguished from its capitalist, imaginary, fetish-dis-
torted expression, because the monstrous theory of the
positive influence of war is based on the confusion of these
two processes—the objective process and the labor process
on the one hand, and the formal process on the other hand.
In fact, from that which has been said it follows that the
form of capitalist profit in the state capitalist regime exhibits the tendency to transform itself into the form of
interest on government securities. These securities represent to a significant degree the right to future real values.
At the same time they can remain in circulation and even
be accumulated in large amounts. But their existence is a
thing in itself, and the objective possibility of realizing
them is another matter entirely. As long as in the process
of war a realization of value takes place as a realization of
incomes, this realization can be designated as either "consumption" of constant capital or as realization of the decreasing sums of surplus value in a new distribution of
surplus value in the direction of big-capitalist groups. A
great amount of the accumulated paper values are tokens
of value whose realization lies in the future and depends
on the one hand on the relations of capitalist reproduction, on the other hand on the existence of the capitalist
system itself. Conceivably, the powerful flood of paper
values in their different forms can become absolutely incommensurate with the real labor process, and will become
under the relations of the *capitalist* structure a sign of its
collapse. In this way, expanded negative reproduction runs
parallel to the accumulation of paper values.

That which has been said above, however, in no way

46

results in the uselessness of the "expenditures" and the negative evaluation of the destructive side of the process from the *capitalist* point of view. Every capitalist crisis whatsoever is a temporary destruction of productive powers. It must be judged, however, from the point of view of the capitalist system by disregarding the *sundry* production cycles. For in the last analysis, every crisis expands the frame of further development of the capitalist system. The same is the case with war. Let us assume that the world war had ended in the second year with the victory of one of the power groups. Without doubt, the capitalist order in such a state of affairs would have had many chances to rise after a period of destruction. After the "wounds had healed," i.e. after relations had been resumed and the destroyed parts of the constant capital had been re-established, the capitalist mode of production would have had the possibility of a certain further development— in a higher, more centralized form than formerly. That *which from the point of view of production cycles directly tied to or closely related to the war presented itself as pure loss, was able to prove to be a temporary decline of productive powers, from the point of view of the general movement of the capitalist system in its great historical scale, at which price a further and thereby more powerful development of these powers had been bought.* In other words, we would then be concerned with one of the *crises* —although with a crisis unprecedented in its dimensions and its form, but by *no means* with a collapse of the capitalist system. The latter, after a certain stagnation, would have continued its development in organizationally more perfect forms.

The question, *crisis or collapse,* depends on the concrete character of the shock to the capitalist system, its depth and duration. Theoretically it is absolutely clear that the process of expanded negative reproduction can only continue to a certain limit, following which a decomposition and a decay of the entire organization begins. We would now like to set about examining this question.

The process of reproduction is not only a process of reproduction of the material elements of production, but also a process of *reproduction of the relations of production themselves.*[32] Expanded reproduction is the expanded reproduction of the given relations of production. Its field, its spatial dimension, becomes larger; the given method of production "expands" by *reorganizing itself internally in its details;* in other words, the reproduction of capitalist production relations reproduces them *fundamentally,* insofar as the relation between capital and wage labor is permanently maintained and expanded. But *within* these relations the details of the production structure are constantly changing; it is sufficient to refer alone to the growth of the so-called "new middle class."

What happens in expanded *negative* reproduction? In order to answer this question, one must remain more thoroughly with the question of the construction of society *in its totality.*

Above all, what are the "production relations," of which we speak?

Marx defines them as the *relationships between people in the process of social labor and the distribution of the products of this labor.* Concretely considered, the following relationships in capitalist society belong here: relations between the capitalist, the foreman, the technician, the engineer, the skilled worker, the unskilled worker, the merchant, the banker, the usurer, etc., whereby the relationships between elements in their *given real combinations*

48

are considered. Consequently, the category of production relations is a general category which pertains to the social structure. To this belong also relationships of a social class character (the relation between workers and capitalists) as well as relationships of another kind (for instance, the relation between two producers, the relation of working together, i.e. the so-called simple cooperation, etc.)[33] Here it must be noted that production relations are not something *different* from the technological organization of labor, insofar as we speak of relationships within the immediate labor process. *In reality,* they fuse with one another. The factory is not only a technological, but an economic category,[34] for it is a complex of social relations of labor and production. Marx introduced the hierarchy of the factory under the command of capital as an example of capitalist production relations. *Technological* elements (the labor power of engineers, directors, mechanics, foremen, workers, laborer) are at the same time elements of *economic organization,* and *insofar as they are tied to a constant circle of persons,* their *social class* character is obvious. This is also comprehensible: classes represent, above all, groups of persons who are united by common conditions and a common role in the production process, with all consequences which follow for the distribution process. The capitalist hierarchy in production is accompanied by the capitalist hierarchy in distribution. These are two sides of one and the same phenomenon which are insolubly connected, fused with one another.

L 29

Production relations are relationships between people as elements of a specific system. But it would be a great simplification if one wanted to deduce from this a specific model of the *relatedness* of these elements. Society is not a *sum* of elements, but at the same time neither is it the

49

arithmetic sum of elements and their connection, for social connection does not stand *next to* the elements. Spatial distribution of persons in the technical labor process and its functional role are accumulated, *frozen* in the personal elements. In this way, social relations transform themselves and find their expression in the "internal structure" of the elements themselves; the model of social connection lives in the heads of the people.

Therefore: the given social structure, the given mode of production, is on the one hand a specific model of connection; on the other hand, these elements are themselves formed by this model.

Everything else is determined by the production relations. The cause of this is easily understandable. If relations of production represented one model of connection and if relationships of another kind (e.g. the state organization) were structured according to a different model, then the system as a whole would have to be absolutely unstable. Capitalist production relations are absolutely inconceivable under the political rule of the working class, and socialist production relations would be inconceivable under the political rule of capital. Consequently, every model of society must inevitably be characterized by a *monism of its structure*, which is the basic condition of existence of every social system.

Capitalist society is to a high degree characterized by this monism. The "constitution" of the factory, of the regiment or of the state chancellery is structured according to one and the same principle, and the hierarchical model of production relations finds its expression in the adequate hierarchy of state power, the army, etc. Above—the class of possessors; way below—the classes of the propertyless; in the middle—a whole scale of transitional groups. The capitalist and the factory manager, the general, the governmental minister or the high official are people of approximately one and the same class, and the character of their functions belongs to the same model, notwithstanding the diversity of their spheres. These functions *cling* to them; they carry, as a result, not only a merely technical but, at the same time, a decided *class character*. The engineer, the officer, the average official are actually again people of one and the same class, and their functions belong to the same model. The small employee (the messenger, doorman, errand boy), the worker, the soldier likewise occupy a similar position, and the hierarchical *class* system confirms itself as a universal principle.

Capitalism is an antagonistic, contradictory system. But the class antagonism which divides the society into two basic classes is everywhere consistently carried out. As a result the structure of capitalism is a monistic antagonism or an antagonistic monism. | L 30

| L 31

We observed the society as a system of elements *in natura*. This point of view must now be carried out in its entire consequences. It is, just as the point of view of reproduction, *categorically binding* for every "critical" epoch and therefore also for the period of the decomposition of capitalism. In "normal" times, i.e. when the conditions of moving equilibrium of the social system are present, one can stay at the level of the fetishistic expression of social relationships, for it possesses a stable character and presupposes specific, quite real, *material*, social labor processes as its base. Money relations, the category of value, etc. are general categories of capitalist economy, and in "normal" times we can make our analysis in these categories, for they are normal for "normal" times; the law of value is the basic condition of the anarchic structure of production, | L 32

51

the *conditio sine qua non* of the flexible equilibrium of the capitalist system.

But things are different when the system of production finds itself in "anormal" relations. That is to say that conditions of flexible equilibrium *are lacking.* Consequently, it is also, methodologically, absolutely inadmissible to undertake the analysis in terms of value relations and categories of fetishized relations at all. On the contrary, one must here take the natural form of things and of labor powers, make calculations in these units, and *regard society itself as the organization of elements in their natural thing-like character.*[35]

This principle was excellently grasped by Rudolf Goldscheid: "In general," he says, "the present war must educate us to one thing above all: to a *deepened natural economic thinking* . . . Nearly all economic questions seem insoluble, if one considers them from the point of view of money economy only but reveal themselves as relatively simple from a natural economic viewpoint."[36]

After all that has been said it will be seen why it is so: capitalist society has become out of joint, and the categories of equilibrium *cannot be adequate for the "critical" epoch.*

The general question is thus now formulated in the following way: What happens to the social system in its natural form, in the form of related natural elements, *under the condition of expanded negative reproduction?*

In the formulas of the value of labor-power we have these series: $c + v + s$; $c + v + (s - x)$; $c + v$; $c + (v - x)$; $(c - y) + (v - nx)$ etc.; parallel to this the value becomes incommensurate with the price. It can easily be seen that from the viewpoint of the capitalist system the situation is not dangerous, as long as the expansion of negative reproduction is at the cost of s. Behind this limit begins, on the one hand, the "consumption" of fixed capital and, on the other hand, the underconsumption of the working class, an insecure functioning of labor power and deficient fulfillment of its *capital-creating* role, i.e. a disturbance in the reproduction of labor power. This process finds expression in two forms: first, in the driving out of labor power from the production process, second, in the reduction of real wages, in the underproduction of energies which create labor power, in the disqualification of the latter, and finally, in the *rending of the connection between the lower and upper elements of the technical hierarchy of production*. The "lower" screws in the capitalist machine, which do not receive enough oil, become loose. Here we see in the rending of cohesions two main forms: 1. their decay and decomposition (e.g., individual resignations, sinking of work discipline, and sloppiness, corruption, ignoring of work rules, etc., among officials); 2. their *revolutionary break* (mass work stoppages, strikes, all kinds of organized insubordination against the capitalist class).

This process of decay of capitalist relations can be perceived at a certain level of expanded negative reproduction; as soon as it has gained ground, it grips all spheres of the capitalist system. The capitalist mentality accumulated in the heads of the lower links of the chain, of obedience to those in power, flees, and its capitalist function becomes impossible. On the other hand, the mentality of the struggle for the preservation of this obedience thickens more and more on the part of the upper links, where technical function coincides with class interest and the most important and most basic class interest corresponds with the interests of preserving the *given* system of production. The latent class struggle, which undermines production relations in the period of *decomposition,* is initiated as open revolutionary struggle at the time of the violent rending of connection of the capitalist apparatus. That which takes place in production is carried through *mutatis mutandis* in the army and in the state administrative apparatus as well.

We have already seen that the process of decay sets in with absolute inevitability after expanded negative reproduction has swallowed social surplus value (s). Theoretical examination can not determine with absolute certainty exactly when, in what concrete number by which this process is characterized, the period of decay begins. That is already a *questio facti.* The concrete situation in the economy of Europe in the years 1918-1920 shows clearly that this period of decay has already begun and that there are no signs of a resurrection of the *old system* of production relations. On the contrary. All concrete facts indicate that the elements of decay and the revolutionary dissolution of relationships advance with every month. Theoretically, this is perfectly understandable. In fact: capitalist society divided into classes can only exist when the mentality of labor peace is so to speak universally valid, in other words, only when and as long as the working class, this most important productive power of capitalist society, silently "consents" to fulfill the *capitalist* function. Once this precondition disappears, the further existence of capitalist society is impossible.

Revolutionary Marxism has precisely determined that in the field of politics the transition of power from the hands of the bourgeoisie to the hands of the proletariat, a transition which is to be understood as a specific historical *process,* finds its expression in a *collapse* of the old state machinery,

54

whereby this machinery decays in its component parts. The state is by no means an object which passes from hand to hand through the different classes and is inherited according to honorable laws of the civil familial code. "The conquering of state power by the proletariat" means the *destruction of* the bourgeoise and the *creation of a new state system,* whereby the elements of the old decayed system are also partly destroyed and partly appear in new combinations, in a new *model of connection.*[37] That was also the point of view of Marx and Engels. The overwhelming majority of the quasi-socialist theoreticians harbored and still harbor a terribly primitive vision of the "conquest of power": the "chief of state," the "government" is replaced, and thereby the "whole apparatus" is conquered.

The revolutionary teaching of Marx was proven correct in this field of relationships not only through abstract observations but also *empirically.*

Much less clear is the transformation process of *production relations.* The concepts which dominated the theory of political upheavals prove to be extraordinarily vital. A typical example in this respect is the observation of R. Hilferding that the "seizure of possession of six large Berlin banks"[38] by the proletariat would provide the latter with the entire industry, *because* in finance capitalist production relations, banks constitute the organizational focal points of the system of technical production, of the "entire apparatus." It has been empirically proven that nothing of the kind takes place, for, in reality, the seizure of possession of the banks merely undermines the commando power of capital. Why? The question is simple to solve. For the reason that the banks "rule" industry on the basis of specific relations of *money credit.* The *mode of connection*

L 35

55

is here the mode of credit connection, and it is just this which collapses when the proletariat seizes possession of the banks.

After all that has been said, it will not be difficult to theoretically comprehend the causes of the decay of the different kinds of *hierarchical* relationships in capitalist society, which are carried out under conditions of expanded negative reproduction.

Most visible is the process of decomposition and later of the revolutionary break in capitalist relations in the *army*. The imperialist army falls into decomposition because— roughly expressed—"the discipline of soldiers decreases," i.e. because the lower links in the chain of the hierarchy no longer are able to serve as links. The revolutionary break in relationships begins with a more or less organized, mass *disorganization* of the "entire apparatus," which is a necessary precondition for the victory of the new class. This disorganization signifies also the collapse of the given system. A "temporary anarchy" is, therefore, objectively considered, an absolutely inevitable stage of the revolutionary process which finds its expression in the collapse of the old "apparatus."

About the same thing happens with the *technical production apparatus* of capitalist society. As we have seen, production relations are at the same time technological relations, and social hierarchy is at the same time a hierarchy in technology. Thus it is absolutely clear that the decomposition and the revolutionary dissolution of the social links of the system as indispensable signs of collapse signify a *decay of the "technological apparatus" of society, as far as we have in mind the technological organization of the people of society.*

But it follows that one *can not entirely* "seize possession"

56

of the old economic apparatus. The "anarchy" in production or, as Professor Grinewetzki characterizes it, the "revolutionary decomposition of industry,"[39] is a historically inevitable stage which no amount of lamentation can escape. Certainly, from an absolute point of view, it would be very good if the revolution and the collapse of old production relations were not accompanied by a decay of technological production relationships. But the sober evaluation of the real processes, their *scientific* analysis, tells us that the period of this decay is historically inevitable and historically necessary.

The decay in the technical hierarchy, which enters at a specific stage of the process of expanded negative reproduction, exercises its pressure on the state of productive powers. Productive powers exist *fused* with production relations in a specific system of social labor organization. The decay of the "apparatus" must, as a result, inevitably be followed by a further *reduction of productive powers.* In this way the process of expanded negative reproduction is *extraordinarily accelerated.*

From the above analysis it follows that upon the base of the bursting (old, capitalist) relationships a "restoration of industry," of which the utopians of capitalism dream, is impossible. The only escape is for the lower links of the system, the basic productive power of capitalist society, the working class, to take a dominating position in the organization of social labor. In other words: only the building of communism is the precondition for a rebirth of society.[40]

L 36

Theoretically, of course, the realization of communism is thereby not yet proven. The question of its preconditions and of the probability of its realization—this question is in no way covered by the question of the collapse of capitalism. Theoretically, a further decomposition is conceivable,

57

a "decline of culture," a regression to primitive forms of medieval, half-natural economy—in short, the picture that Anatole France paints at the end of his *Island of Penguins.* *In the meantime,* we shall push this question aside in order to examine it later. But now we may maintain that a restoration of the *old* capitalist system is impossible. The components of the technical apparatus of production (the personal components) must be taken in *new combinations,* must be related by a connection of a *new kind,* so that development of society is possible. *Mankind faces the dilemma: either "decline of culture" or communism—no third alternative is possible.*

L 37

For the provision that after a series of productive cycles, productive powers begin to grow, a basic precondition must exist: the growth of socialist (moving toward communism) production relations. In this case the "costs of the revolution" (the "deficiency in the labor process" as well as the direct expenditures of social energy in the process of civil war) make up the price for which mankind will buy the possibility of further development.

The communist revolution of the proletariat is accompanied, as every revolution, by a *reduction* in productive powers. The civil war, still in the powerful dimensions of modern class wars, since not only the bourgeoisie, but also the proletariat is organized as state power, signifies a net minus economically speaking and from the point of view of the subsequent *reproduction of cycles.* Nevertheless, we have already seen in the example of crises and of capitalist wars that a consideration from this point of view is a limited consideration; one must examine the roles of the relevant phenomenon, starting with *successive cycles of reproduction in its broad historical scale.* Then the costs of the revolution and the civil war appear as a temporary reduction of productive powers, through which, however, the basis for their powerful development is given by the *restructuring of production relations according to a new basic design.*[41]

The restructuring of production relations has as presupposition: the "power of the proletariat," its "commando" in the state apparatus as well as in the army as part of this apparatus, and in production.

In the process of the struggle for power and of the civil war, in the period of proletarian dictatorship, the curve of productive powers sinks further and further, *at the same time that the forms of organization grow.* This growth of organizational forms occurs under the resistance (above all, so-called sabotage) of the "officers of industry," i.e. of the technicians who do not want to be in a *different* hierarchical system in which they previously were. *But the resistance of this class is much less dangerous for the growing new system than the resistance of the working class for the system of capitalist relationships.* From the point of view of the preservation and development of human society, therefore, only socialist production relations can signify the way out, for only these *are capable of creating the conditions for a relatively flexible equilibrium of the social system of production.*

CHAPTER FOUR
GENERAL PRECONDITIONS OF THE BUILDING
OF COMMUNISM

1. The Model of Relations of Production in the Process of Capitalist Collapse. 2. The Criterion of "Maturity" of Production Relations. 3. The Economic Exhaustion and Decomposition of Capitalism and the Building of Communism. 4. The Building of Communism as an Historical Epoch. 5. The Stages of the Revolutionary Process. 6. Universal Principles of the New Social Organization.

In the previous chapter we saw how naive are the concepts of total and direct transfer of the "old apparatus" onto a new track. An investigation of that segment of the transformation period, which one can label the collapse of the capitalist system, leads us to the statement that the hierarchical, technological system of production, which at the same time constitutes the expression of social class relationships and of relations of production, is inevitably divided into its component parts. No matter how small (in the concretely historical sense) this interval of revolutionary "anarchy" in production may be, it nevertheless constitutes a necessary element in the general chain of development.

However, it must be emphasized that *not all* social-technical bonds are dissolved, but only the bonds of a *hierarchical nature*. At the time of the decomposition of the capitalist system as well as during its revolutionary collapse, ties are broken between the working class, on the one hand, and the technological intelligentsia, the burocracy, and the bourgeoisie, on the other hand. But production relations, in which the relation of worker to worker, engineer to engineer, bourgeois to bourgeois is expressed, are not dissolved; in other words, the general boundary between social classes and the break in the technological apparatus of the organization of persons is carried out first of all in this direction. On the whole, the connection *within the proletariat is not dissolved.* And this connection *constitutes the basic moment of labor socialized in the womb of capitalism.*[42]

The new society can not emerge like a *deus ex machina*. Its elements grow *within the old* society. And since we are speaking about phenomena of an economic nature, i.e. since questions of economic structure, of relations of production, are being touched upon, we must seek the elements of the new society within the *relations of production* of the old society. In other words, the question must be formulated as follows: which form of production relations of capitalist society can in general be placed at the base of the new structure of production?

It is clear that with the answer to this question will also be answered the question of the so-called "ripeness" of capitalist society for its transition through the phase of proletarian dictatorship into communist society. Formerly, the question was raised in a very general and somewhat primitive formulation. That is, the basic criterion of "ripeness," insofar as we mean the "objective" preconditions of the communist social structure, was considered to be the degree of concentration and centralization of capital, also the existence of a specific "total apparatus," and the entire sum of relations of production which complicated the plot of capitalist development of production. However, such a formulation of the question, as it results from the previous investigation, is not sufficient. For it is this very centralized "apparatus" which disintegrates in the process of revolution, and consequently it can not serve *in toto* as a base for the new society.[43]

In the well-known Section 7 of the 24th chapter of the first volume of *Capital* ("The Historical Tendency of Capitalist Accumulation"), Marx emphasizes two basic moments: *the centralization of the means of production and the socialization of labor,* which blossom at the same time with and within the capitalist mode of production.[44] These two moments constitute the *base of the new mode of production,* which has grown up in its interior.

Let us consider these two moments. They constitute parts of the "apparatus," parts of the new organization. Generally considered, every social system is represented as an organization of persons and things. Thereby, the "things" do not constitute simple pieces of external nature but have their peculiar social being. The machine is no machine outside of human society. It only becomes a machine within the system of social labor. From this point of view, society as a system is at the same time an "apparatus of persons and things."[45]

The apparatus of things is the material-technological base of the society. It is not contained in the concept of relations of production but belongs to the productive powers. Even in the process of the revolutionary breaking of

62

production bonds, this apparatus can remain relatively intact. *Its* decay is in no way indispensably necessary. The machines, apparatus, factory installations, etc. naturally suffer during the social upheavals. Nevertheless, the *base* of the shock lies elsewhere. To the extent that a destruction of the apparatus of things takes place, the destruction constitutes mainly the *result of the decay of the apparatus of persons* and the interruption of the labor process. Consequently, the problem exists in the analysis of the second moment, namely in the "socialized labor." The apparatus of persons, which comprehends the totality of labor relationships, includes social groups of which we spoke above. But what appears as *basic form*, as typical and decisive, is the concentration of the proletariat. The "cooperative form of labor," of which Marx speaks, is embodied at the decisive moment in the specific relationships between the workers. And it is here, too, that the focal point of the new society lies.

The total labor power of society, that of the proletariat in purely capitalist society, is on the one hand one of the two components of the concept of productive powers (for productive powers are none other than the total sum of available means of production and of labor powers); thereby labor power, as has already been repeatedly emphasized by the old political economists, is the most important productive power. On the other hand, the interchanging relation between the workers is the basic component of the functioning *apparatus of persons*. Thus it is here that the basic elements of the new structure are to be sought.

And it was thus that the question was conceived by Marx, who saw in the "working class which has been schooled, united, and organized by the very mechanism of the capitalist production process,[46] the basis of future relations of production and also the power which these relations realize."[47]

This sentence is very essential. The "maturing" of communist relations of production within capitalist society is that *system of cooperation which is embodied in the production relations of the workers* and which simultaneously welds the human atoms together into the revolutionary class, the proletariat.

The criterion of "maturity" is therefore that very moment, which is of course a function of the unfolding of productive powers, but which moves into the foreground from the point of view of social organizational technology.

L 39 From this point of view of social organization, the "maturity" of capitalist society is completely understandable, and all considerations of this theme which "refute" it constitute metaphysical nonsense by apologists of capitalism. The existence of a systematic organization within capitalist countries, which is torn by competition, the existence of a system of *state capitalism* at a specific period, is an empirical proof of the "possibility" of the building of communism. In fact, let us abstract for a moment from the concrete historical cover of the process of production and consider it exclusively from the point of view of the internal, abstract logic of production. Here there are two, and *only* two, cases possible: either the socialization of labor allows for the introduction technologically of a planned organization in some kind of concrete social form, or the process of socialization of labor is so weak, labor L 40 "splinters" (according to Marx's expression) to such an extent, that a rationalization of the social labor process is *technologically* completely impossible. In the first case the "maturity" is given; in the second it is lacking. This formu-

64

lation of the question is the *general* formulation of the question for every form *whatsoever* of conscious and formal "socialization." It follows that when capitalism has become "ripe" for *state capitalism,* it is also ripe for the era of the building of communism.[48]

The specific problem of the building of communism is not that the base of social labor is lacking, but that it *consists of a new combination of split social groups* and in the first place that the mental laborers are reclassed in a new system. But this is a theme of a different kind which we will deal with later on. | L 41

The enormous upheaval of the entire capitalist system, which we appraise as its collapse, is considered an argument against socialism by learned and unlearned slanderers from the quasi-Marxist school.[49] This view is logically based on the complete misunderstanding of the *dialectical process,* which is carried out in contradictions. The world war, the beginning of the revolutionary era, etc., *is the very expression of that objective "maturity"* of which we speak. | L 42

Here we see that a conflict of the greatest intensity was the result of the antagonism extended to a maximum, | L 43 which constantly reproduced itself and grew in the womb of the capitalist system. Its earthshaking power is a fairly exact indicator of the degree of capitalist development and | L 44 a tragic expression of the complete irreconcilability of a further growth of productive powers under the veil of capitalist relations of production. That is the very collapse which was repeatedly predicted by the creators of scientific communism. They were right: the concept of a transition to socialism apart from collapse, without disruption of the social balance, without bloody battle, is a miserable reformist illusion.[50]

Once the decay of capitalist relations of production is

L 45 really given and the impossibility of the restitution of the same is theoretically proven, the question arises as to how the dilemma: "decline of culture" or socialism is to be solved. In its basic points, this question has been solved by the previous investigation. In actuality, we saw that the age of the rending of the technological-social strata in production maintains on the whole the unity of the proletariat, *which above all else embodies the material base of the future society.* This decisive and basic element decays in the course of the revolution only partially. On the other hand, it unites itself to an enormous extent, re-educates itself, organizes itself. The Russian Revolution with its relatively weak proletariat, which nevertheless proved to be an inexhaustible reservoir of organizational energy, offers the empirical proof for this.

L 46

"The mathematical probability" of socialism is transformed under these conditions into "a practical certainty."

Nevertheless, one must completely renounce the thought that the indispensable condition for the maintenance and unfolding of the new system, namely the progress of productive powers (a condition which, taken subjectively, represents the class function of the proletariat), begins to realize itself at the very beginning of the revolution. Socialism will have to be *built up.* The available resources of things and persons constitute merely the *starting point* of the development, which encompasses a total powerful *epoch.*

L 47

In the age of the decay of capitalism one can not save capitalism, as we have seen in the previous chapter, because the basic productive power of society, the working class, refuses to fulfill its capitalist, capital-creating function. The basic precondition for the building of socialism

L 48 is the transformation of this capital-creating function into

66

a function of *social labor*. This is only possible under the dominating condition of the proletariat, i.e. under its *dictatorship*.[51] Only with the transformation of the proletariat from an exploited class into a ruling class is the re-establishment of the labor process, i.e. social reproduction, possible.

Within this framework and on this base, the duties which face the proletariat are, on the whole, formally, i.e. independently from the *social* content of the process, the same as those of the bourgeoisie in expanded negative reproduction: frugality with all resources, their systematic utilization, maximal centralization. The exhaustion which results from the war and the interruption of the production process in the period of decay *demands,* from the very point of view of social organizational technology, the transition to socialist relations of production. It is enough to only ask the question generally as to how a system even of only relative equilibrium is possible, or more correctly, how the *creation of conditions of movement towards such an equilibrium* is possible, in order to understand the categorical necessity of the centralized and formally socialized economy. We already saw that the regression of resources of production was one of the main conditions which even within capitalism stimulated a systematic, regulated, organized economy. Therein exists the internal economic logic, which by no means disappears under a non-capitalist formation of production relations, but, on the contrary, makes itself even more noticeable. The *labor process* can not be continued under the rule of the bourgeoisie. Large-scale production can only be expropriated and nationalized under the rule of the proletariat. Economic exhaustion finally stimulates even more methods of rationalizing the social economic process.[52] The totality of these conditions re-

L 49

L 50

L 51

quires the one and only solution to the question: the transformation of capitalism into socialism through the dictatorship of the working class.

We saw that that which makes up a condition of continued existence for society as a whole represents an organizational problem for the proletariat, which it must solve in practice. The proletariat must *actively build up* socialism in this period and simultaneously, in the process of this building, re-educate itself. This task can only be accomplished by means of specific methods, methods of *organized* labor. But these methods have already been prepared by capitalist development.

When the bourgeoisie overthrew the feudalists and when the capitalist mode of production, which had its childhood base in individual private enterprise, forced its way upon the world, the economic process was carried out in an almost absolutely elementary fashion; for it was not the organized community, nor the class subject, which was in action, but rather, dispersed, although to the highest degree active, "individuals." And no wonder that the slogan of this epoch was: *"Laissez faire, laissez passer."* Capitalism was not built: it built itself. Socialism, as an organized system, is built by the proletariat, as organized collective subject. If the process of the rise of capitalism was of an elementary nature, the process of the building of communism is to a high degree a conscious, i.e. organized, process. For communism is created by a class which has grown in the womb of capitalism into that "revolutionary association" of which Marx spoke. The age of the building of communism will therefore inevitably be the age of systematic and organized labor; the proletariat will carry out its mission as a social-technological mission of building a new society which is consciously planned and consciously executed. Simultaneously with the collapse of capitalism, the fetishism of commodities and its half-mystical categories was shattered.[53] "The socialist revolution will set up socialist methods (by no means total socialism all at once), in order to avoid a collapse of the society, to preserve the economic base—and even to extend it. State capitalism saved the *capitalist* state by an active and conscious intervention in production relations. Socialist methods will be a continuation of this active process of organization, but solely for the salvation and unfolding of the *free* society. In the first period they will result only in a new *economics* of the means of production and consumption, will directly *salvage* the society; later they will begin with the *re-establishment of productive powers;* then they will lead to a new, higher *golden age.* In the meantime, stone by stone, link by link, socialism will be built up, as powerful large-scale production and also as a system of newer, simpler, freer social relationships."[54]

What is the "phaseology" of the revolutionary process? This question must be answered. For in the misunderstanding of the legitimate sequence of the different phases can be found a whole series of ridiculous concepts.

A German engineer, Hermann Beck,[55] "refutes" Marx by maintaining that the "social catastrophes (revolutions) are not completely determined economically," for as the example of "antimilitarist" revolutions has shown, the "power displacement" which should be at the very end of the chain of development, here stands at the very beginning." However, it is easy to comprehend which law is at the bottom of the revolutionary process. As a historical *prius* appears the conflict between productive powers and production relations; this conflict finds its subjective class expression in the "indignation of the proletariat," i.e. de-

69

termines the class will in a specific way. The impulse comes from the *sphere of economy* or, more correctly, from the clash between productive powers and economic shell. Further, the catastrophically quick "counter-effect" from the ideological sphere to the productive powers begins; conditions of equilibrium thereby arise on a new base during this process. This dialectic process passes through the following phases:[56]

1. *Ideological Revolution.* Economic conditions destroy the ideology of public peace. The working class becomes conscious of itself as a class which must take over the ruling power. The ideological system of "workers imperialism" breaks to pieces. It is replaced by the ideology of the communist revolution, the "labor program" of coming actions.

2. *Political Revolution.* The ideological revolution is transformed into action, civil war, struggle for political power. Hereby the political apparatus of the bourgeoisie, the entire powerful organization of state machinery, is destroyed. In its place appears a new system, the system of proletarian dictatorship, the soviet republic.

3. *Economic Revolution.* The proletarian dictatorship, in which the power of the working class organized as state power is concentrated, serves as a mighty lever of economic revolution. Capitalist relations of production are smashed. The old structure of the economy ceases to exist. The connections which were preserved are violently destroyed ("the expropriators are expropriated"). The elements of the old system are put into new combinations; in a long and agonizing process, a new model of production relations arises. The foundation of socialist society is laid.

4. *Technological Revolution.* The relative social balance which has been achieved by the reorganization in the struc-

ture of society, assures the possibility of a correct functioning of productive powers, even if originally only on a limited basis. The following step is the revolution in technological methods, i.e. growth of productive powers, the changing and swift improvement of rationalized social technology.

It is obvious that when we speak of these stages of revolutionary development, we mean the focal point of that historical stage, its predominant characteristic, its *typical features*. Within these limits such legitimacy, derived deductively, has again received its first empirical substantiation by the experiences of the Russian proletarian revolution. Failure to recognize the consequence of this period leads to monstrous and theoretically improper conclusions.[57]

Now we must investigate the general principles of the building of communism. It is completely clear that the next epoch must be the epoch of the *dictatorship of the proletariat*, which will *formally* have *similarity* with the epoch of the dictatorship of the bourgeoisie, i.e. will be *state capitalism turned upside-down*, its *dialectical reversal of poles into its own opposite*.

Let us now consider above all the most general conditions of equilibrium for the new base. Present is a strongly damaged material-technological skeleton of production (centralized means of production, partly destroyed by the process of expanded negative reproduction during the imperialist war and the civil war which followed it, and shaken as a result of the ruin of the technological apparatus of persons). Still, this refers to productive powers. In the area of production relations, there are disconnected links, groups in the technological-social, hierarchical scale. As we have seen, the period of collapse does not signify an

71

annihilation of the elements; it signifies an abolition of the connection between them. The elements as such are also partly destroyed (as a result of the civil war, exhaustion, premature consumption, undernourishment, etc.), but it is not this which makes up the basic moment of the period of collapse. One may say that the *connections within the groups,* (between the workers, in the relationships within the classes, between the engineers, technologists, i.e. members of the "new middle class," etc.) are preserved. As we have already stressed, they *grow and gather strength,* in a certain respect, in the womb of the proletariat. In this period the proletariat educates itself, unites and organizes as a class with enormous intensity and speed. The proletariat as the totality of the relations of production constitutes as a result the skeleton of the entire building. But the problem of social organization of production exists in the *new combination of the old elements.* And to be sure, which elements?

It is easy to see that the peak of capitalist society—those who were basically located above production and whose situation in production expressed itself in the fact that they were outside of production (all possible persons of leisure and coupon clippers)[58]—is of no use in the building of the new society; either it is destroyed or must be absorbed by the other groups. The ex-bourgeoisie of an organizational kind and the *technological intelligentsia* under them are a material which is notoriously necessary for the period of reconstruction. It is the social sediment of organizational and technological-scientific experience. It is certainly obvious that these two categories must be regrouped. How and under which circumstances is this possible?

We want to remark, above all, that this is the decisive,

one could say the basic, question for the structure. And it is by no means an accident that in the mature period of the Russian socialist revolution the problem of "specialists" played such an important role.

We know that social ties of a previous kind continued to live on in the heads of persons of this category, in the form of an ideological and physiological sediment. "Healthy capitalism" hovers before them with the tenacity of an *idée fixe*. *The precondition for the possibility of a new social combination of production itself must therefore be the dissolution of the connections of a previous kind in the heads of this technological intelligentsia.*

The process of this "airing out" is exceptionally agonizing and painful. It is accompanied by the partial annihilation of the technological intelligentsia. The latter lead a bitter struggle for the previous model of decaying and violently smashed connections. They resist the *new* model of the combination of social groups of production, for the dominating role is taken here by the *proletariat*. The *technological* functional role of the mental laborers has grown with their advantageous position as a social class group, a position which *à la longue* can be a monopoly position only under the rule of capital. The resistance of this group is therefore inevitable, and in the overcoming of this resistance lies the internal basic problem of the building phase of the revolution. In the basic importance of relations of production within the working class, which continually re-educates itself and *continues* the process of the "formation of revolutionary association," the entire labor is thrown off onto the working class and its own proletarian intelligentsia, which has been educated through the entire course of the revolutionary struggle. The new combination, i.e. the subordination of technological mental laborers to the prole-

73

tariat, is inevitably carried out by means of compulsion on the side of the proletariat and of sabotage on the side of the mental laborers. A relative stability of the system will only be achieved to the degree that accumulated ties of the old kind vanish from the heads of this social category, and the new relationships and the new model of connections are slowly adopted by it.

Here the total sum of newly emerging relations of production must above all be theoretically investigated. For here arises a question of such basic significance: *how is it possible to have another combination of the personal and technological production elements at all when the logic of the production process itself requires connections of a very specific kind?* Must not an engineer or technologist issue commands to the workers and consequently stand *above* them? Just as the former officer in the Red Army must stand above the common soldier. Here as well as there is an inner, purely technical, objective logic, which must be maintained in every societal order whatsoever. How can we reconcile this contradiction?

A whole series of circumstances must be considered here, the investigation of which we want to begin now.

Above all: under the state power of the proletariat and upon proletarian nationalizing of production, the process of the creation of surplus value, as a specific category of bourgeois society, ceases. Technological mental laborers, who in capitalist society fulfilled organizational functions in the production process, were at the same time *socially* the *mechanism of transfer* for the extortion of surplus value as a special capitalist category of profit. It could not have been any different: for the process of capitalist production is at the same time and above all a process of the production of surplus value. The technological mental laborers were

74

therefore means in the hands of the capitalist bourgeoisie and fulfilled their general tasks. Their *spatially determined place* in the social labor hierarchy corresponded to their function as tool for the extortion of surplus value. With the dialectical transformation of the bourgeois dictatorship into the proletarian, the technological function of the intelligentsia was transformed from a capitalist into a social labor function, and the creation of surplus value transformed itself into the creation (under the condition of expanded reproduction) of surplus product, which is utilized for the expansion of the reserve fund of reproduction. Parallel to this, the *basic model of connection* changes, *although the intelligentsia maintains the same "middle" place in the hierarchical scheme,* for the concentrated social power of the proletariat represents the highest state-economic power.[59] On the one hand, the technological intelligentsia stands above the large masses of the working class, but on the other hand, *it submits itself* in the last analysis to the collective will of the working class, which will find its expression in the state-economic organization of the proletariat. The transformation of the process of creating surplus value into a process of systematic satisfaction of social needs *finds its expression in the regrouping of the relations of production, in spite of the formal maintenance of the same place in the hierarchical system of production,* L 52 *which system as a whole mainly bears a different character, the character of the dialectical negation of the capitalist structure* [60] *and which leads, insofar as it destroys the social-caste character of the hierarchy, to the abolition of the hierarchy as a whole.*

Secondly, a *relatively stable* simultaneous existence of the ruling proletariat and the technological intelligentsia occurs, after the latter has *temporarily effectively fallen out*

75

of the process of production. Their return is only secure to the extent that the old accumulated connections vanish from their collective consciousness. Consequently, the new social-technological structure is entered into by intelligentsia who are internally transformed, according to all rules of Heraclitus the Dark. This return is not a repetition of that which has gone before, but a *dialectical process.*[61]

L 53

Third, insofar as a new system of the subjective apparatus arises, these apparatus must—as follows from the whole preceding examination—be based on the *organizations of the working class,* which have become mature in the womb of capitalism and in the tumult of class struggle; these organizations are: soviets, trade unions, the party of the working class which is at the helm, factory committees, special economic organizations which arose after the taking of power, with the relatively numerous cadres of organizational and technologically qualified workers. That is the basic network of general "revolutionary association," which has now risen from below to above. But at the same time it is the milieu *in the pores of which the technological intelligentsia must function.* Formerly, the technological mental laborers and the great bourgeois organizers constituted the basic web of production relations of a higher order, of the system of economic administration (syndicates, cartels, trusts, organs of state capitalist administration). In the proletarian dictatorship the *basic* web is constituted by the different combinations of ascended and newly formed proletarian organizations.

Finally, fourth, the technological intelligentsia begins to lose its social caste character in this system, insofar as continually new groups rise from the midst of the proletariat and gradually place themselves at the side of the "old" technological intelligentsia.

76

In this way the equilibrium of the society is re-established. The domination of the proletariat, which results in its self-education and self-discipline, guarantees the possibility of the labor process, in spite of powerful objective difficulties. The equilibrium in the structure is achieved by new combinations in the personal elements of social production and through subordination of the intellectuals to the top leadership of the proletarian state.

We want to dwell on the general question of the structure of the administrative-economic and administrative-technological apparatus of state power of the proletariat. Under state capitalist production relations, all organizations of the bourgeoisie (syndicates, trusts, cartels, etc.) are subjected to the state power and fused with it. With the destruction of bourgeois dictatorship and the formation of proletarian dictatorship, these administrative apparatus are also destroyed. The organizations of trusts, the state organs of regulation of the old society, etc. decay. As a rule (theoretically we have proven it in the last chapter) they can not be taken as "entire apparatus." But this does not mean that they have not fulfilled their historical role, for the entire, most highly complicated total series of these sometimes very subtle organizations, which encompass all of social economic life with their feelers, played, taken objectively, the role of the screw, which increased and accelerated the process of centralization of the means of production and of the proletariat. On the other side, upon the decay of these apparatus, their materially technological, objective skeleton remains. And, looking at the question on a general scale, just as the proletariat takes first of all the centralized means of production, i.e. the materially technological bone-and-muscle-system of capitalist production, which mainly finds its expression in a system of machines and as Marx said in a "vascular system"[62] of apparatus, likewise does the proletariat seize not the personal element but the *essential element* of the old administrative system (buildings, chancellories, offices, typewriters, the entire inventory in general, books by which one can orient himself more easily, and finally all possible materially symbolical devices, such as diagrams, models, etc.[63] After it has seized these along with the other "centralized means of production," it builds its apparatus, the base of which is made up of the *workers organizations.*

The working class has at its disposal the following organizations: the *councils of workers delegates,* which transform themselves from a tool for the takeover of power into tools of the government; the *party of communist overthrow,* the *spiritus rector* of proletarian action; the *trade union associations,* which transform themselves from tools of the struggle against the employers into organs of the administration of production; the *partnerships,* which are transformed from means of the struggle against commercial transaction into an organization of the state apparatus for the purpose of general distribution; the *factory committees* and similar organizations ("factory councils" in Germany, "workers committees" and "shop stewards committees" in England), which transform themselves from local organs of the workers' struggle against the employers into elements of the general administration of production.

The network of these, as well as of *totally new* organizations *specially created* on their base, constitutes the organizational ground floor of the new apparatus.[64]

Under the given conditions we have before us above all a dialectical *change of functions* of the workers organizations. It is completely clear that it can not be otherwise with the *transposition* of relations of domination, because

L 54

78

the working class, which has seized state power, must inevitably become the power which appears as *organizer of production*.[65]

Now we must raise the question as to the general principle of the system of organization of the proletarian apparatus, i.e. as to the interchanging relationships between different forms of the proletarian organizations. It is clear that the same method is formally necessary for the working class as for the bourgeoisie at the time of state capitalism. This organizational method exists in the coordination of all proletarian organizations with one all-encompassing organization, i.e. with the state organization of the working class, with the *soviet state of the proletariat*. The "nationalization" of the trade unions and the effectual nationalization of all mass organizations of the proletariat result from the internal logic of the process of transformation itself. The minutest cells of the labor apparatus must transform themselves into agents of the general process of organization, which is systematically directed and led by the collective reason of the working class, which finds its material embodiment in the highest and most all-encompassing organization, in its state apparatus.[66] Thus the system of state capitalism dialectically transforms itself into its own inversion, into the state form of workers socialism.

No new structure can be born before it has become an objective necessity. Capitalist development and the collapse of capitalism have led society to a dead end, have halted the process of production, the base of existence of society. The renewal of the production process will only be possible under the domination of the proletariat, and therefore its dictatorship is an objective necessity.

A stability of the emerging new society can only be achieved with the greatest possible union, contact, and

79

working out in common of all organizational powers. And therefore that general form of labor apparatus, of which we spoke above, is so necessary. Out of the bloody passion of war, out of the chaos and the ruins, out of misery and destruction, arises the structure of the new, harmonic society.

CHAPTER FIVE

CITY AND COUNTRY IN THE PROCESS OF SOCIAL TRANSFORMATION

1. The Process of Negative Expanded Reproduction and Agriculture.   2. Production Relations and Agriculture. 3. State Capitalism and Agriculture.   4. Collapse of the Capitalist System, City and Country.   5. Preconditions of Socialism in Agriculture and General Principles of the Building of Socialism.

"The foundation of every division of labour that is well developed, and brought about by the exchange of commodities, is the demarcation between town and country. It may be said, that the whole economic history of society is summed up in the movement of this antithesis."[67]

This Marxist characteristic must be taken into consideration more than ever in the transitional period. For if in the "normal" period of capitalist development, i.e. in a relative proportionality, given in advance, between "city" and "country," insofar as we are speaking about the distribution of social productive powers which is necessary for the equilibrium of this system—if in this period the process of production can be considered in its abstract form, as a

L 55

81

process of the production of value and surplus value—then this is no longer sufficient.

The *naturalistic* point of view gains a decisive significance, and the division of social production into different spheres of "concrete" labor and, first and foremost, into industry and agriculture thereby takes on exclusive importance. The growing incongruity between these branches of the economic system has also emerged before the war; the imperialist search for an "economic supplement," i.e. for an agricultural base for the industrial countries, actually constitutes an outlet for that contrast between "city" and "country" of which Marx spoke—but already on a world scale.[68] The problem of *raw materials*—the basic problem of the present time—and the problem of *supply* are the most topical problems. This all forces us to consider the question of city and country as one question requiring a special examination.

Above all, we must pursue in which way and means the *process of expanded negative reproduction* has expressed itself in agriculture.

Let us first consider the process in isolation. It is self-evident that the same phenomena are perceived here as well as in industry. War takes away a huge quantity of productive powers: it regroups the labor powers and diverts them from productive labor; it robs agriculture of inventory, of animal labor power; it reduces livestock; it decreases the quantity of fertilizer; it diminishes the area for sowing. By drawing away labor power, which in agriculture plays a relatively greater role than in industry (for the organic composition of capital is deeper here), it narrows the base of production and reproduction. The narrowing of the base of production finds its expression in the decrease of created products. That is the general picture.

But the process of agricultural reproduction, considered in its reality, is not an individual and isolated reproduction process. *It is a part of the general process* which presupposes an "exchange of material" between city and country. Insofar as we talk about the reproduction of the means of production, agricultural production is dependent on the conditions of reproduction in industry (machines, tools, artificial fertilizer, electric energy, etc.). Expanded negative reproducttion in industry intensifies the analogous process in agriculture. And vice versa, the reduced amount of consumer goods, which constitute the elements of reproduction of labor power, intensifies for its part the process of expanded negative reproduction in industry. As a unified process, expanded negative reproduction expresses itself in the decreasing amount of created products (all the means of production and consumer goods).

The diminishing of the base of production is paradoxically expressed in a rise of the money "rentability" of agriculture.[69] | L 56

The rise in price for agricultural products, however, entails just such a rise in prices (as a rule an even greater one) for industrial products. But agriculture in wartime quickly freed itself from debts, accumulated capital in money form, and piled up stores of products. As Professor Lederer quite correctly notices, this contradiction finds its explanation therein that the colossally inflated prices for industrial products were the function of such a diminution of their real amount that agriculture could not drive them up at all. From this follows that the base of production in agriculture has preserved itself better than the base of production in industry, that agriculture in spite of the process of expanded negative reproduction disposes in reality of, relatively speaking, much greater amounts of

83

products than does industry. That is a fairly essential distinction, which must also express itself in the period of the fall of the capitalist system.

The essential difference, however, is the *economic structure* of this most important branch of production. A peculiarity of this structure is the exceptional *motleyness* of economic models, which reflects and expresses *the relatively weak degree of socialization of labor*. On the whole we can single out these categories: large-scale capitalist agriculture which is based on wage labor; capitalist ("Kulak,"* "large-estate owner"), which likewise uses wage labor and is based on it; the "self-employed" farm economy which does not exploit wage labor; and finally the small farm system of the half-proletariat. The different combinations in relationships between the *subjective elements* of these models provide a very heterogeneous picture. In the framework of large-scale capitalist economy, we perceive about the same social hierarchy of production as in industry: the economic constitution of the latifundium is, on the whole, the same as that of the factory; above—the capitalist producer, lower—the main manager (director); then a staff of qualified mental laborers (economists, bookkeepers, etc.); still lower—the "employees"; under them the skilled laborers (for agricultural machines, on the supply roads, at the electrical power stations, etc.) and finally the unskilled laborers. Relations within the economy of the large-estate owner, where the scale of production is usually limited to two categories, are different; the master and his workers. The "self-employed" economy knows no hierarchical step-ladder. The economy of the half-proletariat constitutes in its composition of personnel the lowest step

* Literally: "The Fist," a popular expression for the village moneylender.

84

in the ladder of another economy—the latifundium, the factory. We saw in previous chapters that the basic moment which determines the possibility of a *direct rationalization* of production constitutes socialized labor (in any form whatsoever, whether state capitalist or socialist). It is therefore clear that even the system of state capitalism alone, in relation to agriculture, must take on a somewhat altered "form of organization."

It goes without saying that the need of the bourgeoisie to adapt agriculture to the system of state capitalism was nothing less than enormous. For agriculture is—especially at the moment of violent disturbances—a decisive branch of production: without coats, electric lamps, and books, one can still live, but one cannot live without bread. The army may be poorly shod, but it cannot exist from the nourishment of St. Anthony. The moments which motivated state capitalist organization were present, therefore, to an aggravated degree. And at the same time the direct possibility of the rationalization of production was especially weak.

How was this problem solved by capitalism?

In two ways: first *by nationalization of one sector of large production units; second by indirect regulation of the production process through the circulation process.*

From the preceding we can fairly clearly see the relative "weakness" of the first method. Of course, the capitalist state already had at its disposal several branches of agricultural production (e.g. state forests), but it did not have such bases of support, as for example, industry has in the trusts. For this reason the extent of direct bourgeois nationalization of *production* was relatively slight and was executed usually in the form of various "communalizations" and "municipalizations." An importance so much the great-

85

er was gained by the second method: the regulating of production by *regulating the process of circulation or by organizing distribution.* The state monopoly on grain, the ration system for agricultural products, the forced delivery of products, the ceiling prices, the organized supplying of industrial products, etc., etc.—all this finally directed development *in the direction* of nationalization of production. Here we perceive a regressive model of development, the beginning stages of an organizational process, which, just as in industry, had as its starting point the process of circulation (corners, rings, syndicates).

L 58

In this area the state capitalist system was able to rely on syndicate-like agricultural associations of a special kind, especially on *cooperatives.* By regulating the circulation process, the mechanism of agricultural production on the whole was also regulated, even including the small individual farm. The system of "free trade" with agricultural products was finally undermined. Of course, the specific conditions of agriculture, the high specific importance of the small and medium commodity-producing farms, produced great difficulties here too; this expressed itself in the "illegal," "free" markets and in speculatitve trade; but nevertheless, as long as the system of state capitalist organization *as a whole* was strong, agriculture was also adapted to the *universal* apparatus, the main component of which was organized industry.[70]

L 59

From this arises the thesis: *insofar as the collapse of the system of state capitalism has as starting point the disintegration of relations of production in industry, it also signifies the collapse of this system in relation to agriculture.*

The stagnation of state capitalist apparatus expresses itself here in its constant puncturing by the black market in agricultural products. The revolutionary tearing of connections furthers in the first period—*separation between city and country.*

In the epoch of state capitalism one can distinguish three kinds of ties between city and country: 1. connections of money credit, which are of a finance capitalist nature (mainly through bank institutions); 2. state and communal apparatus of organization; 3. the real exchange process between city and country themselves, which is carried out partly by apparatus of organization and with the help of these, and partly without these. Now let us observe what must inevitably and unavoidably happen, when the proletariat seizes power, in the sphere of relationships between city and country.

The bonds of money credit and finance capitalist connections are totally, irrevocably, and for ever broken in the power seizure by the proletariat. In the power seizure of the banks, credit relations go to the devil, and one can no longer speak of a "restitution of credit," for the entire basic system of customary relationships is penetrated, every "confidence" has disappeared, and the proletarian state represents itself to bourgeois consciousness as a collective bandit.

State and communal apparatus likewise disintegrate in their component parts, along with the disintegration of almost all state mechanisms of the old model. That apparatus which expressed the hegemony of industry over agriculture and the hegemony of the city over the open country (in capitalist form), ceases to exist as a closed system of organization.

Finally, the *real exchange process,* in which the unity of the "national economy" expresses itself, recedes enormously in its dimensions. After a thorough analysis of the decay of capitalist industry, it will not be difficult to grasp the

L 60

87

cause of this. Even the process of expanded negative reproduction undermined the base of exchange during the imperialist war by reducing to a minimum the quantity of products put out by the city, i.e. the real equivalent of products needed by the country population. With the collapse of the capitalist apparatus of production, the process of production stagnates almost completely: one lives from old stockpiles, from remnants, which have been saved by the war and which the proletariat has inherited. The money which in "normal" times seemed to be a self-value finally turns out to be a symbol of mediation without independent value. For the persons who must dispose of the masses of agricultural products, almost every stimulus for delivery of the products into the city is lost. *The economy of the society decomposes into two autonomous spheres: the hungry city and the open country, which—despite the partial destruction of productive powers—disposes of fairly large stores of "surpluses," for which the market is not available.* The decomposition of the entire social system of production reaches its peak. This phase of the "economic history of society" is expressed in the singling out of the two main species of social labor—a circumstance in which a further existence of society becomes impossible.

Still, before we go over to the examination of the conditions of the *new equilibrium,* we must examine those basic forms which are assumed by the collapse of the capitalist system within the "open country."

L 61 Here the following thesis is surprising: during a relative stability of the "open country" and the existence of a considerable mass of products, the process of decomposition in the relationships within agricultural production must take place considerably more slowly; on the other hand,

88

insofar as a multiplicity of economic forms is available, as is alien to large-scale capitalist industry, insofar will the form of the transformation process in all its phases be different from the process which we examined in the previous chapters.

Let us first take large-scale capitalist agriculture. Here the process of the breaking of ties reminds us above all of that which takes place in industry. However with several modifications. First, it is executed here more slowly than in the city. This happens because in agriculture, where consumer goods are created on the very spot, the under-consumption by the working class does not manifest itself in such a crass form. The system of partial payment in kind effectively guarantees the reproduction of labor power, and consequently, the stimulus for the dissolution of the ties between the subjective elements of the system is considerably weaker. Second, the proletariat is here not nearly as "schooled" by the mechanism of the capitalist production process. Its composition (half-peasant elements), the work methods (the seasonal character of the work, a much larger spatial separation in the labor process, etc.)—this all inhibits its "ideological revolutionization" and the working out of a "revolutionary work program." These factors, however, delay only the general line of development, but they do not negate it. The influence of the city and of the organizations of the industrial proletariat gives the external push to the intensification of the process, which develops independently, and finally the break in capitalist production relations is inevitable, a break which is carried out in the same direction as that in industry.[71]

But the break in rural relations of production is carried out in different directions. This is determined by the spe-

L 62

cific structural singularities of rural economics. As we have seen, one sector of the mechanism of personnel (the half-proletarian owners of small farm lots) constitutes the lowest link in the capitalist hierarchy; the other elements (the middle farmers) are not only "competitors" of large-scale agriculture in the market: they also frequently serve as an object of exploitation in a veiled and hushed-up form of exceptionally complicated and multiple relationships (tenant farming, usury, dependence on rural banks, etc.). Here we have a form of lower and middle elements of the labor hierarchy, which form has no place in the purely capitalist scheme and does not represent socialized labor but, so to say, follows closely its example. Nevertheless, its specific importance is very great, insofar as we consider the entire social scheme in its concrete totality. This character of relationships of production, since the supported lower links of the system consist of a large number of independent farms, also determines the model of decomposition which is expressed *in a struggle between the farms,* i.e. in the battle between the laboring farms and half-proletariat on the one hand and the large farmers and half-estate-owners on the other hand. Concretely considered, the combination of struggling elements can be very manifold, according to the specific importance of the various agricultural models, according to the variations of these models. (For these are very fluid transitional categories with an enormous number of shadings, etc.). Taken *in itself,* isolated from the entire remaining economic complex, this break of connections harbors in itself also the possibility of a return to more primitive forms, for the active power here is constituted by the very split labor of the small owners, and not by the socialized labor of the proletarians. But *in*

L 63

90

the given historical complex the break constitutes one component of the universal collapse of the capitalist system.[72] That is the *peasant rural revolution,* whose significance is that much greater the less that capitalist relations have been developed. This struggle may be, and usually is, accompanied by a great waste of energy and a splitting of the material base of production (a certain division of the large goods, of the inventory,[73] of livestock, etc.), i.e. by a *further reduction of productive powers.*

Now the question arises: *how is the new equilibrium possible*—on the one hand the equilibrium *within* agriculture itself and on the other hand the equilibrium *between city and country?*

This question is decisive for the fate of humanity, for it is the most important and most *complicated* question.[74]

We have already seen that the universal model of the *new* equilibrium must be the inverted model (the dialectical negation) of the equilibrium in the relations of the state capitalist system.

Let us consider above all the process *within* agriculture.

The rending of the ties between the various subjective elements of *large-scale capitalist agriculture* must be replaced by the organization of these elements in a new combination. Actually, the problem here is of the same kind as in industry. However, it is complicated by two moments: first, by a partial destruction of the large-scale capitalist farm as a large-scale farm at all; second, by a much slighter degree of maturity of the rural proletariat itself. The first is inevitable in the struggle for the land on the part of the peasantry. It is understandable that the size of the concessions fluctuates strongly according to the specific importance of the peasantry in general and its distribution

91

in the various categories. The second moment produces a much larger amount of frictions within the organization; the process of self-education of the proletariat goes more slowly.

As far as equilibrium in the remaining sphere of agricultural production is concerned, it has the tendency to base itself on an equalizing redistribution of the land as the starting point of development. It is evident that this condition, taken independently from the development in the cities, would have to provide the impulse towards a new capitalist cycle of "American" stamp. This possibility, however, disappears with the liquidation of the commodity economy in the city and with the socialist organization of industry. The inevitable result of the dictatorship of the proletariat is therefore a *latent or more or less open struggle between the organizing tendency of the proletariat and* L 64 *the anarchical tendency in commodity production on the part of the peasantry.*

In which forms, however, can the organizing influence of the proletarian city be determined? And how can a new equilibrium *between* city and country be achieved?

Obviously the real process of "exchange of material" between city and country can serve as the only firm and secure base for the decisive influence of the city. The *renewal of the process of production in industry*, the restitution of L 65 industry on socialist formula constitutes therefore the necessary condition for a more or less swift incorporating of the village into the process of organizing.

But since the rebirth of industry is determined itself by an influx of food into the cities, there results the absolute necessity of this influx *at any price*. This minimal "equilibrium" can only be achieved (a) *at the cost of a part of the*

92

resources left over in the cities and (b) with the help of *state-proletarian coercion.* This state coercion (requisition of the grain surplus, natural taxation, or other forms) is economically founded: first, directly, insofar as the peasantry itself has an interest in the development of industry which delivers agricultural machines, tools, artificial fertilizer, electric energy, etc.; second, indirectly, insofar as the state power of the proletariat represents the best means of protection against the re-establishment of economic pressure of the large-estate owner, of the usurer, of the banker, of the capitalist state, etc. Consequently, state coercion here is not "pure application of force" à la Dühring and insofar constitutes a factor which progresses along the main line of universal economic development.[75] Insofar as the industrial proletariat relies on the formally socialized (nationalized by the proletariat) large-scale farm, it directly organizes the process of *production.* The lack of agricultural inventory may also motivate one sector of the farmers to unite (agricultural communes, cooperatives). But for the main mass of *small producers,* an incorporation into the process of organization becomes possible chiefly through the sphere of circulation—that is, formally in the same way as in the system of state capitalism.[76] The *state and communal* (which latter should theoretically not be opposed to the state) *organs of distribution and acquisition* constitute the basic apparatus of the new system of equilibrium.

Here the question arises of those peasant organizations which in the period of capitalist development were already welded together by the dispersed producers in the process of circulation, i.e. the question *of economic cooperatives.* From the analysis of the decomposition of the capitalist system in agriculture, we saw that small production in the

L 66

L 67

L 68

L 69

93

process of this decomposition preserved its relative stability. Naturally, the agricultural cooperative exhibited the tendency to transform itself into agricultural syndicates, at the peak of which stood capitalist large-estate owners, and did even transform itself in part into these. Thus far the apparatus of cooperatives also turned out to be damaged. Even so it is clear that certain forms of the cooperative had to perish—that is the fate of the *credit* cooperative. But at the same time it is without doubt that the stability of the farm economy must find its expression in a relative stability of the apparatus of cooperatives of the farmers as well. What is its further fate? Does it disintegrate, as the syndicate and the trust inevitably do? Or not? Before we answer this question, we must examine another basic problem more precisely: the struggle between the proletariat and the peasantry, as class agents of the various economic models.

"The basic powers and basic forms of the common economy are capitalism, small-scale production of commodities, communism. The basic powers are: bourgeoisie, petit bourgeoisie (especially the peasantry), and proletariat."[77] Farm economy remains as usual the small-scale production of commodities. "Here we have an exceptionally wide, very thorough-going and firmly anchored base of capitalism. On this base, capitalism is preserved and celebrates its rebirth in the most severe struggle with communism. The forms of this struggle are the black market and speculation, which direct themselves against state acquisition of grain (as well as other products), and in general against state distribution of products."[78] The struggle against or for the commodity market, as a hidden struggle around the models of production—that is the economic milieu in the relationships between city and country, which milieu on the whole arises

94

after the conquest of power by the proletariat. Here is a great difference from that which occurs in the city. In the cities the main struggle for the economic model *ends* with the victory of the proletariat. In the open country this struggle is ended as far as a victory over large-scale capitalism is concerned. But in the same moment it experiences —in other forms—a *rebirth* as a struggle between the state program of the proletariat, which embodies socialized labor, and the anarchy of commodities, the unrestrained speculation of the peasantry, in which the dispersed property and market elements are embodied. But since simple commodity production is nothing other than an embryo of capitalist economy, the struggle between the aforesaid tendencies is a continuation of the struggle between communism and capitalism. However, since two "souls" live in the breast of the farmer, and since the poorer he is, the greater specific weight the proletarian tendency has, the struggle is complicated still more by the internal struggle within the peasantry itself.

L 70

L 71

How is this situation reflected in the fate of the apparatus of cooperatives of the peasantry? It is clear that things are different here from industry. The apparatus of cooperatives can waste away (in a growing retrogression of exchange ties between city and country); it can be destroyed (in the prevalence of "kulaks" in the village and in the intensification of the struggle between them and the proletariat); it can be absorbed by the universal socialist organization of distribution and gradually rebuilt (in the resumption of the real process of exchange of products and the decisive *economic* influence of the cities). Consequently, a complete decomposition of the apparatus is theoretically not absolutely necessary.

L 72

In this way the new equilibrium arises in uninterrupted

struggle, and therefore its restoration is so slow and painful. The process is carried out more rapidly, the faster reproduction in industry is restored and the faster the proletariat sets about its more important task: the *technological* revolution, which completely changes the conservative forms of economy and provides a powerful impulse towards the socialization of agricultural production. But this belongs to the theme of the following chapter.

CHAPTER SIX

PRODUCTIVE POWERS, EXPENSES OF THE REVOLUTION, AND TECHNOLOGICAL REVOLUTION

1. The Concept of Productive Powers. 2. Productive Powers and Social Reproduction. 3. Productive Powers and Crises. 4. Productive Powers and Wars. 5. Productive Powers and Revolutions. 6. Proletarian Revolution as the Necessary Condition for Elimination of Capitalist Contradictions. 7. Expenses of Proletarian Revolution. 8. Forms of the Expenses of Proletarian Revolution and Retrogression of Productive Powers. 9. The New Social Equilibrium and the Technological Revolution. 10. Methods of Technological Revolution. 11. Technological Revolution, City and Country.

In the third chapter we touched generally upon the question of productive powers and the expenses of the revolution. Now we need to examine this question in detail, since everything depends upon its evaluation. For it is the productive powers of the society, their niveau and

97

their *movement,* which in the last analysis determine the total complex of social phenomena. And the stability of that equilibrium in the structure, i.e. the equilibrium between the different personal groupings of society, tthe subjective groupings of the social system, has its foothold in a specific equilibrium *between society and the external milieu,* in an equilibrium, the character of which is determined by the stage of development of the material productive powers of society. But first we must answer the question: what are the productive powers?

In "Poverty of Philosophy," Marx[79] wrote: "Thus it is slapping history in the face to want to begin by the division of labour *in general,* in order to get subsequently to a specific instrument of production, machinery. Machinery is no more an economic category than the bullock that drags the plough. *Machinery is merely a productive force.* The modern workshop, which depends on the application of machinery, is a social production relation, an *economic* category." (*Italics* by us. N.B.)

By productive powers Marx obviously means here the objective and personal elements of production, and correspondingly the category of productive powers is not an economic but a technological category. On the other hand, we find in Marx another definition of productive powers. In Volumes I and III of *Capital,* Marx very often uses the expression "productive powers" wholly in terms of "productivity of social labor."[80] But while Marx labels productivity of social labor as productive power, he repeatedly refers to the fact that labor power is the basic productive power of the society.

However that may be, it is clear that if one is able to operate at the first stage of the examination with an indefinite concept, later on the inexactitude of this concept makes itself felt.

Above all: wherein does the meaning of this concept lie? If one speaks of productive powers, one wants to thereby signify the degree of domination of human beings over nature, the degree of the mastering of nature. Mainly by this means is the degree of achieved development finally determined. From this point of view, one must above all consider the question of the relationship of Marx's definitions to each other. Rodbertus recommends keeping these two concepts strictly apart. In his work, *On the Illumination of the Social Question,* he writes: "Productive power and productivity are to be distinguished. Productivity means the effectiveness or fruitfulness of productive power. If instead of 10 workers, 20 workers are employed, instead of one machine of a certain degree of effectiveness, two of the same are set up, then the productive power has risen once again as high; if 10 workers produce as much as 20 formerly, or if a machine which costs no more than another has, however, twice the degree of efficiency of this one, then the productivity has risen once again as high. Here, too, labor is the ultimate criterion. Larger sums of work mean greater productivity."[81] From this formulation of the question, the cause for the "indefiniteness" of the concept of productive powers is fairly clear: it is namely a *border concept,* which stands on the line between technology and economics. In respect to *economics* the concept of the efficiency of social labor is important. In respect to technology, the material equivalent of this efficiency of social labor is significant, i.e. the existing total sum of means of production and of labor powers. Therefore we are able to speak of productive powers and of

L 76

99

productivity as of two sides of one and the same mathematical magnitude M : (a + b), where M is the entire mass of products which are expressed in some kind of units of use effect (whether it be energy magnitudes or something else is in this case irrelevant); a and b are units of social labor: a—units of dead labor, b—of living. If one considers this formula from the "objective" point of view, we have (1.) the amount of various kinds of products, (2.) the amount of various kinds of means of production, and (3.) the amount of various kinds of qualified labor powers. These three magnitudes are absolutely dependent upon one another; thereby the means of production represent the primary element. The means of production decompose into means of labor and other means of production (raw materials, resources, etc.). These two parts are for their part organically bound to each other. The concrete means of production presuppose an adequate amount of qualitatively determined labor powers, for the process of production has its technological logic, and in that given moment the objective and subjective elements are joined according to a very specific model and in a very specific relation. But on the other hand, the means of production even in their objective specificity decompose into two parts, which mutually determine one another. From this point of view we are able to consider as the starting point of the analysis the active part of the means of production, and to be sure the means of labor, *the technological system* of society. This system constitutes, as Marx expresses it, "the true graduators of the progress of productive powers."

Therefore, if we speak of the progress or retrogression of productive powers of society, we mean the rising or falling of social labor productivity; if we speak of the distribution of productive powers, we mean the distribution and redistribution of means of production and labor powers; if we speak of the physical annihilation of productive powers we speak simultaneously of the annihilation of means of production and labor powers; if we need a sociological definition of productive powers, we can take *the technological system* of society, the active, changeable "factor" of social development.

Such a mutual dependence of the elements of the formula

$$\frac{M}{a + b}$$

where a and b mean the amount of all existing means of production and/or all labor powers, presupposes, however, a "normal" course of social reproduction, i.e. a condition of fluent, movable equilibrium. The technologically given proportionality of these magnitudes (and consequently also the possibility of substituting one magnitude for the other) disappears with a disturbance of the social equilibrium. The productivity of social labor expresses itself as usual in the formula $M : (a + b)$, but a no longer means the *total* existing means of production, b not *all* existing (i.e. to be exploited) labor powers, and the relation between a and b, which under normal relations is a given, technologically determined magnitude, *ceases to be such.*

The dynamics of productive powers is tied to the dynamics of production, i.e. to the process of reproduction. The objective and subjective elements of productive powers (complex of means of production and labor powers) are reproduced in this process *in natura,* in order to become active factors of this process. From the point of view of reproduction, one must therefore regard the formula $M : (a + b)$ from the side of the factors a and b, i.e. the objective and subjective elements of the process of produc-

101

tion. Thereby *a* and *b* are not isolated complexes but magnitudes which are *organically united in the labor process.* Only insofar as they participate in the labor process do they constitute direct components of productive powers.

The development of productive powers does not represent a constantly rising curve. On the contrary, it must already be *a priori* clear that in an antagonistic society, in a society based on anarchy of production and social anarchy, *an uninterrupted development of productive powers is impossible.* For in such a society the laws of equilibrium are exclusively realized in the course of constant or periodically recurring disturbances of equilibrium and can only be realized in this fashion. Consequently, the restitution of equilibrium must have its disturbance as starting point. But since every disturbance of equilibrium, the functional meaning of which consists in this case of its restitution on a broader—but simultaneously more contradictory—base, is inevitably united with a decline of productive powers, it is self-evident that in *the antagonistic society a development of productive powers is only possible in the course of their periodic disturbance.*

This is expressed very clearly in capitalist crises. "The world trade crises must be regarded as the real concentration and *forcible adjustment* of all the contradictions of bourgeois economy."[82] (emphasis ours—N.B.)

This "forcible adjustment" of contradictions, i.e. the creation of conditions for a new equilibrium, is accompanied by a disturbance of productive powers. The new equilibrium reproduces the old contradiction on an expanded base, etc. From this point of view, therefore, the process of capitalist reproduction is not only a process of expanded reproduction of capitalist production relations: *it is simultaneously a process of the expanded reproduction of capi-*

talist contradictions.[83] The new equilibrium is established every time by way of the "destruction of a mass of productive forces," and, to be sure, in increasingly rising dimensions. In the *"Theories of Surplus Value,"* Marx gives an excellent analysis of the most important forms of this destruction, and from two points of view: the really objective (the natural form) and the fetishist-capitalist (the value form).

"When speaking of the *destruction of capital* through crises, one must distinguish between two factors.

"In so far as the reproduction process is checked and the labour-process is restricted or in some instances is completely stopped, *real* capital is destroyed. Machinery which is not used is not capital. Labour which is not exploited is equivalent to lost production. Raw material which lies unused is no capital. Buildings (also newly built machinery) which are either unused or remain unfinished, commodities which rot in warehouses—all this is destruction of capital. All this means that the process of reproduction is checked and that the *existing* means of production are not really used as means of production, are not put into operation. Thus their use-value and their exchange-value go to the devil.

"Secondly, however, the *destruction of capital* through crises means the depreciation of *values.* . . . This is the ruinous effect of the fall in the prices of commodities. It does not cause the destruction of any use-values. What one loses, the other gains. . . . As regards the fall in the purely nominal capital, State bonds, shares etc.—in so far as it does not lead to the bankruptcy of the state or of the share company, or to the complete stoppage of reproduction. . . . it amounts only to the transfer of wealth from one hand to another."[84]

But since the reproduction process is destroyed "in general," even in the latter case, a destruction of capital in its objective form takes place here, too. On the other hand, the centralization of capital, accelerated by crises, creates a "higher form" of further movement, and the further development is bought at the *price of a transitory and partial destruction of productive powers, i.e. at the price of a reduction of their niveau.*

The same phenomenon is actually perceived in the examination of *capitalist competition,* which is based on the splintering of social production. If one were concerned with a reasonably regulated system, then labor would distribute itself between individual branches and enterprises in the necessary relation. In capitalist society there is no such conscious regulator. Therefore the law of equilibrium —the law of value—functions as an elementary law, like "the law of gravity when a house falls about our ears." But just for this reason, because it is a blind law of social elementary powers, it is realized by *constant disturbances.* Herein the disturbance of equilibrium constitutes the indispensable condition of the establishment of a new equilibrium, which is followed by a new disturbance, etc. The mechanism of these vacillations, i.e. of the constant disturbance of equilibrium by which equilibrium is constantly realized, is the *mechanism of competition.* From this it follows that the development of productive powers in capitalist society is bought at the price of its constant waste. This waste (the "costs of competition") is the necessary condition of the forward development of the entire capitalist system. For every new link in the chain of flexible equilibrium reproduces this equilibrium in a higher form, due to the centralizing process.

L 79 | From this point of view one must also consider war,

which is nothing other than a method of competition at a specific level of development. That is the method of *combined competition between state capitalist trusts*. The expenses of war are thus actually nothing more than the expenses of the centralizing process. From the point of view of the capitalist system as a whole they play a positive role insofar as they do not lead to the collapse of the system.

L 80

Stated generally, one can consider the crises as well as competition from three points of view: from the point of view of those links in the chain of the process of reproduction, since a reduction of productive powers takes place; from the point of view of reproduction of the respective system of production, since a transitory retrogression of productive powers constitutes the condition itself for their further progressive movement; from the point of view of the collapse of the old system and a social transformation, since the old system is exploded by its contradictions and the expenses of collapse transform themselves into the expenses of the revolution.

These expenses of revolution can be considered for their part either *sub specie* of those cycles of reproduction, since a destruction of material productive powers takes place, or *sub specie* of the transition to a new, more productive social structure which eliminates the contradiction between the development of productive powers and the "chains" in its structure. That a transition to a new structure which represents a new "form of development" of productive powers is inconceivable without a transitional falling of productive powers, must in itself be clear. And the experience of all revolutions, which from the very point of view of the development of productive powers had a powerful, positive influence, shows that this development was bought at the price of an enormous plunder-

L 81

ing and destruction of these powers. It is not possible any other way, insofar as we speak of revolution.[85] For in the revolution, the shell of production relations, i.e. the personal apparatus of labor, is exploded, and this means, and *must* mean, a disturbance of the process of reproduction and consequently also a destruction of productive powers.

If that is so—and it is absolutely so—then it must be *a priori* evident that the *proletarian* revolution is inevitably accompanied by a strong decline of productive powers, for no revolution experiences such a broad and deep *break* in old relationships and their *rebuilding* in a new way. And nevertheless, the proletarian revolution constitutes from the very point of view of the *development* of productive powers an objective necessity. This objective necessity is provided by the fact that the economic shell has become *inconsistent* with the development of productive powers. *World productive powers are not compatible with the state-national structure of society, and the contradiction is "solved" by war. War itself becomes incompatible with the existence of the basic productive power—the working class—and the contradiction can only be solved—really solved—by revolution.*[86]

The working class alone, the basic productive power of society,[87] can *save* this society and provide the impulse for its further development. But it can only do it at the price of sacrifices which are unavoidably evoked by the resistance of the exploded capitalist "shell," which is personified in the *capitalist bourgeoisie.*[88] The extent of the expenses of proletarian revolution is determined by the depth of communist revolution, through the *principal* change in the structure of production. In bourgeois revolutions such principal change did not occur, for private property, as a legal expression of a specific kind of production relations, con-

L 82

106

stituted the base of precapitalist relationships as well. Correspondingly, social equilibrium was achieved after the revolution in the sphere of the economy by some improvements over that which existed previously, and in the sphere of politics by the transition of power from the hands of *owners* of one kind to *owners* of another kind. Consequently, it is *a priori* evident that here such a decay, which is inevitable in a principal radical breach of old relationships, does not appear and can not appear. This breach constitutes an indispensible law of proletarian revolution.[89]

All *actual* costs of revolution are based on a *diminution of the process of reproduction* and a decline of productive powers. By their *form*, they can be divided into several rubrics.

I. *Physical annihilation of elements of production.* Under this belong the annihilation of means of production (of factories, machines, railroads, apparatus, livestock, etc.); annihilation of persons—workers, etc.—in the process of *civil war* and *class war* between the proletarian state and the bourgeois state; annihilation of machines and other means of production and their damage as a result of the poor treatment, sabotage, delayed repair of specific parts, etc.; annihilation of technological mental laborers (in the civil war, in the general results of the shock, etc.)

It is clear that on the one hand we are concerned with annihilation of material-objective elements of production and on the other hand with annihilation of elements of persons.

II. *Disqualification of elements of production.* Under this belong the depreciation of machines and means of production in general; the (physical) exhaustion of the working class; the disqualification of the labor power of the technological mental laborers; the resorting to "surro-

107

gates" in the means of production and labor powers (a larger percentage of women, of non-proletarian and half-proletarian elements, etc.).

L 83 III. *Decay of the connection between elements of production.* Under this belong the decay, already extensively examined above, of the hierarchical system of labor of capitalist society, the social split, the disturbance of every equilibrium, which is followed by a temporary *stagnation of the process of reproduction;* under this belong also the dissolution of the cohesion between city and country, the decay of relationships between states, etc. In the process of this decay, not only the *personal* elements of the universal apparatus of labor, but also the *material-objective* parts fall from actual production: if machines, their "system," entire factories "stand still" they are effectively lost. *Productive powers are not physically annihilated here, but they take on the position of potential productive powers. They exist in natura, but they exist outside of the process of social reproduction.*

The decay of the connection between the elements of production is the *main cause* of the decline of productive powers in the transitional period. It is tied to the transformation of the structure of society, and seen in reality, inseparable from it; the decay results *inevitably* from this transformation and therefore must stand in the focal point of theoretical examination. Other expenses as well must also be figured into the actually rebuilding, like for example the original *inability* of the working class to grasp the elements of production, the "blunders" of the period of reconstruction, etc., i.e. all the energy applied to the restructuring of the social apparatus of labor with *all the faux frais of this process.*

IV. *The regrouping of productive powers in terms of unproductive consumption.* Under this belong above all the satisfaction of the needs of civil war and of socialist class war. With the growth of the revolutionary process into the revolutionary *world* process, the civil war is transformed into a class war, which is led by a regular "red army" on the part of the proletariat. It is completely clear that the expenses of this war will beget just such economic exhaustion from the point of view of the next cycles of reproduction as the expenses of every other war. It *can* be waged because upon the new base a process of structural *organizing* takes place. But the retrogression of productive powers as a result of the process of expanded negative reproduction continues as long as the war does. This war not only demands material objective resources: it requires also the best human material, the administrators and organizers among the workers.

L 84

It is easily seen that in each of the mentioned cases the result is a diminution, a deficit, a stagnation and meanwhile also a laming of the *process of reproduction,* which is equivalent to a decline of productive powers. To "deny" this would be just as imprudent as if one were to "deny" the process of revolution itself. The question now arises wherein the functional significance of this decline exists. The distinction between the short-sighted ideologists of the bourgeoisie and the ideologists of the proletariat does not exist here in the fact that the first ones "confirm" these facts and the others deny them, but rather that the ideologists of the bourgeoisie conceive these phenomena statically, while the only correct (and as a result universally valid) method exists in considering the transitory fall of productive powers *from the point of view of the process of transformation,* i.e. not only from the point of view of *following* cycles of social reproduction but from the broad point of view of large historical dimension.

It is self-evident that if the process of the retrogression of productive powers has its expression in the direct annihilation of elements of production, it proceeds that much more painfully the more that productive powers have declined during the war. The retrogression of productive powers as a result of this cause unites with its "revolutionary" decline: in the process of social transformation, war and revolution fuse with each other, as the explosion of the capitalist system.[90]

From the entire previous analysis it follows that a restraining of the breakdown of productive powers can not appear before there appears a new social structure, a new social equilibrium in production. This is the most necessary condition of all for the resumption of the process of reproduction. Not until after the rebuilding of the human labor apparatus, the rebuilding which eliminates barriers towards the development of productive powers and explodes the "shell," which has been transformed from "forms of development" into "chains of development"—only after this will the last phase of the revolution be possible: the *technological revolution,* the revolution not of relationships between human beings but of relationships between the human community and external nature.

First there will have to be a period of "primitive socialist accumulation."[91] Wherein existed the essence of *capitalist* primitive accumulation in production? In the fact that the political power of the bourgeoisie mobilized powerful masses of the population after they had plundered them, transformed them into proletarians, and made the basic productive power of capitalist society out of them. *The pro-*

duction of proletariat is the "essence" of the period of primitive accumulation. "In the history of primitive accumulation, all revolutions are epoch-making that act as levers for the capitalist class in course of formation; but above all, those moments when great masses of men are suddenly and forcibly torn from their means of subsistence, and hurled as free and "unattached" proletarians on the labour-market."[92] In this way *capital,* by plundering, class rape, and robbery, mobilized the productive powers after it had made them a starting point of further development.

But socialism too, which grows up out of the ruins, must inevitably begin with the *mobilization of living productive power.* This labor mobilization constitutes the basic moment of socialist primitive accumulation, which is the dialectical negation of capitalist primitive accumulation. Its class meaning does not exist in the creation of the preconditions of the process of exploitation but in the economic rebirth with an *abolition* of exploitation, not in the rape of a handful of capitalists but in the self-organization of the working masses.

L 85

We already saw that the process of decay of the capitalist system not only resulted in the annihilation of living labor power or its disqualification, but also simply in its *elimination* from the labor process. Therefore it is completely clear that as soon as the proletariat begins with the re-establishment of the process of reproduction, it must begin with the mobilization of powers which have fallen out of the process of production. But it must not limit itself to these. At the first level of development, because the proletariat takes over the strongly damaged material-technological skeleton as inheritance, living labor power gains a special importance. Therefore the transition to a system of *universal compulsory labor,* i.e. the inclusion also of the

L 86

111

broad, *non-proletarian masses*, above all of the peasantry, is a peremptory necessity in the proletarian-state labor process.[93] The rise of a collectively operating, living mass-productive-power constitutes the starting point for further work. The most important sphere of labor is originally transportation, the supplying of fuel, raw materials, and food.[94] Here begins the *rising* line of development, which will be accompanied by a powerful development of *technology*. The abolition of private property of the means of production, the abolition of the "right" to patents and of business secrets, the unity of the program, etc. make possible the transition to electrical application of energy. If under capitalism private ownership of land with all its "supplements" (waterfalls, rivers, peat-deposits, etc.) and the monopoly of capitalist cliques enormously inhibited the development of productive powers and if even in the most powerful capitalist countries the application of electric energy, the building of new power stations, etc. clashed with the limits[95] set by private property, during the domination of the proletariat a true technological revolution, a revolution in social production technology, will follow the period of "primitive socialist accumulation." "The age of steam is the age of the bourgeoisie, the age of electricity is the age of socialism."—This is an absolutely correct technological characteristic of the beginning stages of developing socialism.[96]

The electrification of industry, the construction of huge power stations, the creation of a powerful net of transportation, will radically change the relation between city and country. This will not only require the transformation of splintered small owners into social laborers, it will rationalize and radically transform the entire process of agricultural production. The primitive, almost barbaric tools

112

will be replaced by the latest achievements of technology, and thereby the basic incongruity of capitalist production, the incongruity between the development of industry and the development of agriculture, will be lifted, that incongruity which was determined by the existence of ground rent and private possession of land and which led even before the war to a powerful inflation of prices for agricultural products.[97] The contrast between city and country will gradually disappear, and with it at the same time the specific "idiocy of country life" will disappear. Productive powers of human society will be distributed in the various areas according to the most fitting natural conditions (proximity of sources of raw materials and fuel, etc.). The question of the "location of industry" will now be solved, independently from the existence of capitalist limits, and the development of productive powers will make giant strides forward, slowly but surely.

CHAPTER SEVEN

GENERAL FORMS OF ORGANIZATION
IN THE TRANSFORMATION PERIOD

*1. State Capitalism.   2. System of Socialist Dictatorship.
3. Socialization.   4. Nationalization.   5. Municipalization.
6. Other Forms of Socialization.*

Bourgeois political economics abstracts "principally" from the *historically social forms* of the process of production. Therefore, the relations of domination, of exploitation, of class character of the given social formation, etc. are "inessential" to it. It is evident that this is "principally" nothing other than the elevating to a "principle" an enormous theoretical confusion, which is effectively of definite advantage for the bourgeoisie. This confusion achieved its greatest intensity during the war and in the postwar period. It was expressed above all in the crudest mistaking of the system of *state capitalism* for the system of *socialist dictatorship of the proletariat.*

Werner Sombart defines socialism in his introduction to "Foundations and Critique of Socialism"[98] in the following way: "Socialism is practical social rationality of antichrematistic tendency." This, by your leave, "definition" has its roots deep in literature. For there exists an old tradition, which has acquired the determination of a prejudice, a

114

tradition which throws into one pot the slaveholding "communism" of a Plato, the Prussian-Junkerian "state socialism" of a Rodbertus, the finance-capitalist state capitalism of the war period, and Marxist communism, for the simple reason that all these forms exhibit a "social rationalization of anti-chrematistic tendency." However, it is clear that such a point of view is in no way superior to those barbarically crude, naive, but also clever definitions which were given during the war to imperialism as an extra-historical, indeed even generally biological function.[99]

This confusion logically comes from the fact that the class character of the state is veiled here, which appears under the name of the "universal," the "whole," the "social whole," and other pretty words, and that the specific character of production relations is suppressed. These are merely considered from the angle that the anarchy of production and the money system related to it are eliminated. But since one can fit into this formula all possible forms of economic structure which have been constructed on the basis of natural economic and simultaneously systematically regulated relationships, *whatever character these relationships may have within or without the classes,* it is clear that this formula is worthless because it is too general, because it encompasses social structures which are directly *opposed* according to their class characters.

If we now go over to state capitalism, we shall see that state capitalism is a completely specific and purely historical category, in spite of the fact that it exhibits a "social rationality" as well as an "anti-chrematistic tendency." For it constitutes at the same time a species, the "most perfect" species of *capitalism.* The basic relation of production in the capitalist order is the relation between the capitalist who owns the means of production and the worker who

L 88

115

L 89　sells his labor power to the capitalist. It is impossible, indeed absurd, to ignore this basic class characteristic in a consideration of state capitalist structure. From the point of view of interchanging relations of social powers, state capitalism represents the power of the bourgeoisie, *raised to a higher exponent,* where the domination of capital achieves its ultimate power, a truly enormous strength.[100]

L 90　In other words: *state capitalism is the rationalizing of the process of production based on antagonistic social relationships and on the domination of capital, which has its expression in the dictatorship of the bourgeoisie.*

L 91　Since state capitalism is a growing together of the bourgeois state with capitalist trusts, it is evident that one can speak of no kind of "state capitalism" in the dictatorship of the proletariat, which in principle excludes such a possibility.[101]

"Generally" speaking, one could raise the question of the possibility of such a form, since the proletarian state from the beginning of its existence regulated the activity of the capitalist trusts *before the "expropriation of the expropriators"* and "reasonably prepared" this expropriation, in order to preserve all "apparatus" intact. If such a system were possible, it would not be state capitalism, for the latter presupposes a capitalist state. This would not be the high-

L 92　est expression of the capitalist order but a certain intermediary step in the development of the revolution. But

L 93　such a form is *impossible,* for its presupposition is based on the illusion, to be sure a very wide-spread illusion, that the proletariat could "seize possession" of all capitalist apparatus without violating their capitalist virginity, and that the capitalist masters could with pleasure comply with all instructions of proletarian power. Consequently, a condition

116

of equilibrium is presupposed under conditions which *from the outset preclude any equilibrium.*[102]

The *system of socialist dictatorship*, which one could label "state socialism" if that designation were not compromised by its customary usage, is the dialectical negation, the opposite of state capitalism. The *model* of relations of production is radically altered here; the supreme power of capital in production is eliminated, because the foundation of all foundations of the capitalist order, the relations of property, becomes another. Here a "social rationalization of anti-chrematistic tendency" is present. But these traits are based on a totally different class relation, whereby the entire character of the process of production becomes totally different. In the system of state capitalism the economically-active subject is the *capitalist state*, the collective total *capitalist*. In the dictatorship of the proletariat, the economically active subject is the *proletarian* state, the collectively organized working class, "the proletariat organized as state power." In state capitalism, the production process is a process of production of surplus value which falls into the hands of the capitalist class, with the tendency to transform this value into surplus product. In the proletarian dictatorship, the production process serves as a means of systematic satisfaction of social needs. The system of state capitalism is the most perfect form of exploitation of the masses by a handful of oligarchs. The system of proletarian dictatorship makes any kind of exploitation whatsoever inconceivable, for it transforms the collective capitalist property and its private capitalist form into collective *proletarian* "property." Therefore, according to its essence, in spite of the formal similarity, the diametrical opposite is provided.[103] This opposite also determines the opposition of

L 94

L 95

L 96

L 97

117

all functions of the systems under consideration, even when they are formally similar. Thus, for example, universal compulsory labor in the system of state capitalism means an enslavement of the masses of workers; whereas in the system of the proletarian dictatorship it is nothing other than the self-organization of labor by the masses; the mobilization of industry is in the first case an intensification of the power of the bourgeoisie and a stabilization of the capitalist regime, while in the second case it is a stabilization of socialism; all forms of state compulsion represent an extortion in the state capitalist structure which secure the process of exploitation, extend and deepen it, while state compulsion in the proletarian dictatorship represents a method of the building of communist society. In short, *the functional oppositionality of formally similar phenomena is totally determined by a functional oppositionality of systems of organization, by their opposed class character.*[104]

Communism is no longer a form of the transitional period but its completion. This is a classless and stateless structure which is constructed completely harmonically in all its parts. For the first time the absolutely uniformly organized "totality" emerges. The dictatorship of the proletariat "matures" on the path of evolution into communism and dies out along with the state organization of society.

The transition from capitalism to socialism is completed by the concentrated power of the proletariat—the lever of proletarian dictatorship. The system of measures by the help of which this transition is completed is usually termed "socialization."[105] From that which has been said it is already clear that this term is not completely exact. If one speaks of socialization in the sense that the labor process as a whole satisfies social needs, i.e. the needs of the whole

118

society, then such a "socialization" was there even in the framework of capitalism. Marx meant especially this when he spoke of "socialized labor." Rodbertus maintained the same thing as well, when he established the thesis that the essence of society was communism. However, it is clear that in this context we are speaking of something else. Here we are concerned with those measures which are supposed to create a new model of production relations *based on a radical change in relations of ownership.* In other words: "expropriation of the expropriators" must also constitute the contents of the process which is socializing itself. Consequently, by socialization is meant the transfer of means of production into the hands of society. However, here there appears a certain inexactitude of the label. For in the transition period between state capitalism and communism, the economically active subject is not the "total society," but the *organized working class,* the proletariat. Nevertheless, if we consider the process in its totality, having begun with the violent expropriation up to the dying out of the proletarian dictatorship—which is also a *process*—the difference between the proletariat and the totality of social laborers becomes smaller and smaller, and finally disappears entirely. Therewith, the justification for the term "socialization" is also provided.[106] If we mean by socialization transfer of means of production into the hands of the organized proletariat as the ruling class, then the question arises as to the concrete forms of this transfer. Essentially we have already examined this question in the previous chapters. Those concepts must only be defined here which have continually been muddled by the opponents of communist revolution. It is clear that to the extent that the economically active subject in the transitional period

L 100

L 101

L 102

119

makes up the working class constituting itself as state power, in so far does the basic form of socialization of production represent its *etatization* or *nationalization*.[107] However, it is obvious that the etatization (nationalization) contains "in general" a completely different material class content, according to the class character of the state itself. If one does not—as the representatives of bourgeois science do—regard the state apparatus as an organization of neutrally mystical nature, then one must comprehend that all functions of the state also bear a class character. It follows that one must keep strictly separate *bourgeois* nationalization and proletarian nationalization. Bourgeois nationalization leads to a system of state capitalism. Proletarian nationalization leads to a state form of socialism. Just as the proletarian dictatorship is the negation, the antipode of bourgeois dictatorship, proletarian nationalization is the negation, the complete opposite of bourgeois nationalization.

The same must be said of the different kinds of municipalization, communalization, etc. Theoretically, it is incorrect to the highest degree to *oppose* these concepts to the concept of nationalization. For the system of so-called "local self-administration" is in *every class society* whatsoever (consequently in a society where the state exists) nothing other than a component part of the local apparatus of state organization of the ruling class.[108] A specific class character of state power creates just as specific a class character of the local organs of this power. One must therefore keep strictly separate proletarian municipalization and bourgeois municipalization, as with different kinds of "nationalization."

It is self-evident that besides these basic forms, where the proletariat as totality directly captures the process of

120

L 103

L 104

L 105

production, a series of lesser forms of this same process is present (with special reference to the rural population). Here the connection with the proletarian state is slighter, but it is there. For the proletarian dictatorship is that lever which overturns the old order and builds a new one. In the last analysis, therefore, the socialization process in *all* its forms is a function of the proletarian state.

CHAPTER EIGHT

SYSTEM OF THE ADMINISTRATION OF PRODUCTION UNDER THE DICTATORSHIP OF THE PROLETARIAT

1. The Class Character of the State and Methods of Administration.   2. Proletarian Administration of Industry in the Period of the Destruction of the Capitalist System.   3. Proletarian Administration of Industry in the Critical Period ("Militarization").   4. Administration and Schooling in the Administration in Different Phases of the Process of Transformation.   5. The Probable Course of Development.

L 106

Under the domination of capital, production is production of surplus value, production for the sake of profit. Under the domination of the proletariat, production is production for the satisfaction of social needs. The different functional significance of the entire process of production is provided *by the distinction in property relations and in the class character of state power.*[109] Theoretically the concept is completely wrong that a specific class is bound to a single form of administration, unchangeable in its details. Any social class can find itself in different conditions, to which the methods and forms of administration must be

122

adapted. These latter are determined by norms of technological expediency; at the same time, the *different* forms
have one and the same class content, if specific property
relations and a specific class character of state power are
given.

The praxis of the bourgeoisie can serve as the best example. The bourgeoisie in the age of imperialism has gone
from the forms of "extensive democracy" to a curbing of
the rights of parliament, to the system of "small cabinets,"
to the strengthening of the role of the president, etc. But
did the curbing of the "rights of parliament" and the "crisis
of parliamentarianism" also signify a curtailment of the
rights of the bourgeoisie and a crisis of its domination? Not
in the least. On the contrary, these phenomena characterized a strengthening of the domination of the bourgeoisie,
a centralization and militarization of its power, which was a
categorical necessity in the epoch of imperialism from the
very point of view of the bourgeoisie.

When Spencer held that the "industrial state" in essence
must be anti-militarist, because militarism represented a
specific characteristic of the feudal regime, he was deeply
in error, for he elevated the peculiarities of a *phase* of capitalist development to a universal form. World competition,
which put the entire development under the sign of war,
forced the bourgeoisie to change the form of its domination. But only vulgar minds can view in this an encroach-
ment upon the rights of the bourgeoisie in favor of a non-
existent quantity. One does not dare *oppose* even the so-
called "regime of persons" to class domination. On the contrary, in a specific combination of relations, class domination is able to find above all in the very regime of persons
its corresponding expression. Thus, for example, the domination of large-estate owners, who found their expression

L 107

123

in absolutism. Thus the bourgeois dictatorship in the period of civil wars, since it finds its most complete (i.e. adapted to the conditions of the moment) form in the dictatorship of the saber. The change in the *form* of administration can also take place in the sphere of industrial administration, according to technological expediency.

But if these principles are correct at all, then they are also correct for the period of proletarian dictatorship.

With that it becomes clear that the different systems of industrial administration in the process of social transformation must be observed in strict dependency upon the concrete *phase of development*. Only by this method of observation can one grasp the necessary sequence of forms and the inevitable variations of different administrative systems in the framework of the *constant "class essentiality"* of the given system.

The original phase of development is the period of the *decomposition and the breakdown of capitalist production relations and simultaneously the period of the seizure of possession of strategic intersections of economics by the proletariat.* In general, this period sets in earlier than the "transition" of political power to the proletariat, because the stages of revolution (their ideological, political, economic, technological levels) are not sharply set off from one another, and one period flows over into the other. The struggle for socialization of production, i.e. for the proletarian factory, occurs all along the line, from the bottom upwards, parallel to the growth of the revolutionary wave. This struggle has its expression in the fact that the old system is riven and finally split by such organizations as the revolutionary "workers committees" (Russia), "workers councils" (Germany), or other similar representative or-

124

gans of the working class uniting in the course of the struggle. This phase of development must be analyzed first of all.

In the period considered, society finds itself in a condition of the highest instability. The interchanging relation between social powers is such that an equilibrium on the old base is absolutely impossible. The capitalist bourgeoisie and the technological mental laborers, who as a rule march along with the capitalist bourgeoisie in this period, have no particular interest "in repairing production." Their aim is directed towards preventing the victory of the working class. The factories become more and more "without a master." The aforesaid organizations of the proletariat constitute the first attempt to insert a new "master"—the working class. Is this system of wide-spread camaraderie, of workers councils, the most *technologically* perfected? Certainly not. But its functional role exists not at all therein. In the period under consideration, we have the first steps towards establishing a new equilibrium, *without which* any building of really more perfect forms is inconceivable. Even in "normal" capitalist periods, the bourgeois organizers of production regarded the problem of the interchanging relation between the organs of the capitalists and those of the workers to be one of the most important problems of administration.[110] This problem *can not be solved* here *at all*. One can only speak of a probing towards a *new* system of equilibrium. At the given level of development, one can not therefore list "perfect technological administration" as an immediate task at hand at all. The mastering of this task presupposes a certain stability of the elements of production, not only the objective-material elements but *also the subjective (personal) elements*. But in the period under

125

consideration this precondition does not and can not exist. However, in a certain sense one can still speak of a step forward here too.

In actuality we saw above that technological personal relationships in labor are at the same time social relationships. Therefore, from the point of view of comparison with the absolute disorganization of the economic apparatus, since every principle of organization is lacking in the enterprise, the "take-over of power" in the factory by the proletarian germ cell represents a plus, even from the point of view of the logic of "pure production." This take-over of power appears immeasurably more essential in reference to its role in the universal historical process. For only in this way can the penetration of the working class as an organizing principle in the process of production take place. The task is by nature an economic task of *struggle:* to

L 108 strengthen the working class as ruling class in all pores of economic life. In respect to technology, this system, which inevitably results in the most thorough-going collegiality, the principle of absolute eligibility (thereby this eligibility sails under the political flag and not under the flag of the technological order), the frequent replacement, and—on the strength of the extensive collegiality—a decentralization and splintering of responsibility—this system is far from perfect.[111] But the working class can only stabilize its positions in economic life by calling to life the lower cells of its administrative apparatus, cells which swiftly unite with each other, grow together with the organizations of the working class which were ripened while still in the "womb of capitalism" and *in this way create the new web of the proletarian economic apparatus.* Decomposition of the old

L 109 apparatus and rough draft of the new one—that is the model of administration of production which we observe.

126

It would be appropriate here to introduce the analogy with the process carried out in the army. In place of the strictest imperialist subordination appears the principle of far-reaching eligibility: countless committees are formed in all links of the chain of the apparatus of the army; the issues of the army become the object of the most extensive consultation and discussion; the "old power" in the army is finally discredited and buried; the new organs and through them the new classes become actual nodal points of power. What is the objective meaning of this process? The first and most important: *the decomposition, the destruction of the old imperialist army.* Second: *schooling and preparation of active organizational powers for the future proletarian army, a schooling which is bought at the price of the destruction of the old system.* No one can maintain that the regimental committees make the army able to fight. But the objective task does not exist in supporting the old army's ability to fight. On the contrary, it exists in the destruction of this army and the preparation of the powers for a *different* apparatus.

However, notwithstanding all the similarities of the processes here and there, there also exists a great distinction between them. In production, a great *constancy* of the entire process is maintained. That is because, in the internal capitalist system, the *base* of the apparatus of production of the future, primarily the trade unions, had already been given. Corresponding military organizations were non-existent, however,—*had* to be non-existent. Therefore, development in the army proceeds in leaps and bounds, the entire process expresses itself more crassly, more roughly, one would hope in a more revolutionary manner. | L 110

Totally different from the case under consideration is the model of *proletarian-militarized production.* The "mili-

127

tary" model of any organization first appears on the program when the system finds itself in a critical situation. In war, there is always a constant threat to the individual parts of the struggling apparatus (the army) as well as to the "totality." Therefore, as a result of the conditions for the existence of this organization itself, a specific model of this organization is required here: the greatest exactitude, the unconditional and undisputed discipline, speed in decision-making, unity of will, and therefore minimal consultation and discussion, a minimal number of councils, maximal unanimity. On the other hand, however, insofar as the elements of the organization are not internally welded together and do not carry out all decisions themselves, the army is based on a system of measures of force which reach their maximum in this very area and find their crassest expression right here.

The latter element has to be particularly strong when the army is recruited from elements who *themselves* have no interest in war, when war is waged *against* their interests. Such a war is the imperialist war. But even under the domination of the proletariat, the element of necessity and the measures of coercion play a large role, so much the greater the percentage on the one hand of not purely proletarian elements and on the other hand of unconscious or half-conscious elements among the proletariat itself.[112] In

L 111

this case the "militarization"[113] of the population—above all in the organization of the army—constitutes a method of *self-organization of the working class and the organization of the peasantry by the working class.*

Insofar as the proletarian dictatorship and its classic model—the soviet form of the state—finds itself in a critical situation, insofar is it also clear that it must assume the character of a *military-proletarian* dictatorship. This means

128

that the business apparatus of the administration shrink, comprehensive corporations are replaced by narrow ones, all existing organizers and administrators from the working class are distributed in the most frugal manner.

The same phenomenon—in intensified form—arises necessarily upon the danger of an *economic* catastrophe. This danger is created by economic exhaustion during the imperialist war and the civil war. As far as the emphasis of proletarian tasks is transferred to the area of economic construction, where the basic web of economic apparatus is *already* penetrated by administrators from the working class, where workers organizations have *already* become the base, the matrix of these apparatus, a restructuring of these apparatus can be perceived with absolute certainty, a restructuring which moves in the direction of the decrease of camaraderie and in some cases (in individual factories, etc.) to the introduction of the individual administration. This latter signifies neither a curtailment of the rights of the class nor a diminishing of the role of its organization. This is the *form* of proletarian administration of industry, compressed and consolidated,—a form which has adapted to the relations of quick working, to the "pace of war." In respect to technology, this form is far more perfect, for its significance does not exist in the fact that the old is destroyed or that only the domination of new relations is assured and the masses are educated; the emphasis rests here in the very enlargement of the social apparatus, in a constant and exact process of labor. This task is solved by the revolution, *after* the base of the proletarian apparatus of administration has been created at all. Here one no longer needs to concentrate his aim on the problem of stabilization of the class position of the proletariat—this question is essentially solved; here the emphasis does not

129

rest on the principal change of relations of production but in the discovery of such a form of administration which guarantees maximal efficiency. The principle of far-reaching eligibility from below upward (usually even by the workers within the factories) is replaced by the principle of painstaking *selection* in dependence on technological and administrative personnel, on the competence and the reliability of the candidates. At the top of the factory administrations appear responsible persons—workers or specialists. But they are elected and placed by the economic organs of the *proletarian* dictatorship; they are nominated and recommended likewise by workers organizations. Within this system, no engineer may fulfill a different function from that required of him by the proletariat.

This model of proletarian administration of industry is only possible and expedient under specific conditions: above all it presupposes a stability of the already existent soviet power and the presence of a certain social equilibrium on a new base. Such a system would be impossible and inexpedient in the first phase of revolution, in the phase of the destruction of old connections and the takeover of the vital points of production. This must be emphasized with utmost decisiveness.[114]

Another question must be touched upon. It is connected to the question already examined: namely the question of the relation of the methods of *administration* to the methods of *schooling for the administration*. One of the most important tasks of the soviet regime in general is the educating of the broadest masses for direct administrative labor. The question is the same if we speak of the *economic* organizations of the state apparatus. In the first period the function of schooling *fuses* with the function of the administration itself. It could not be otherwise. The

130

bourgeois organizers of production, the technological mental laborers, go against the proletariat then; the workers still have no administrative experience, but everything is thrown upon their shoulders. In this situation, the vanguard of the proletariat administers as it learns, and learns as it administers. There is no *other* solution at the first level of the building of socialism. But for the fulfillment of these tasks, the very form of a widely executed system of camaraderie is useful. This is not so much a kind of administration as it is much more a *school* of administration. However, it is evident that one must not make a virtue out of necessity. In further phases of development, insofar as the positions of the working class as ruling class have stabilized themselves and insofar as a secure foundation for a competent administration of industry has arisen, the base of which is already a group of selected worker-administrators; insofar as, on the other hand, the technological intelligentsia turns back like the lost son into the process of production—insofar does the function of administration *separate* itself from the function of schooling for this administration. The learning of administration is no longer bought at the price of constant errors in administration itself. Increasingly broader masses become interested and learn industrial administration in special posts and acquire the specific methods and practices much more systematically than was possible in the previous phase.[115]

What is the probable course of further development on the way to communism? As far as the intensity of the economic crisis (the crisis of exhaustion) lets up and increasingly larger amounts of human material are accumulated, which are in a position and able to administrate, one will also no longer need the sharply delineated military model of administration. With all its absolute advantages,

131

it also has certain great disadvantages which arise from the model of coercive discipline. It is unconditionally necessary under conditions where one must act swiftly and decisively: then its disadvantages disappear before its advantages. But if it has fulfilled its commission, it is succeeded by a new phase of the "unfolded" system of administration which represents in no way a simple repetition of the stage already gone through, but a synthesis of the two preceding stages. Then, speaking with Hegel, the first phase will be the thesis, the second the antithesis, and the third their fusion in a higher unity. Development will of course not thereby stand still. To the extent that state power and every compulsory regulating of human relationships die out, communist humanity will create the highest model of *objective* administration," where the problem of camaraderie or of individual persons, no matter in what form, will itself disappear, for people in the future will do voluntarily that which the dry results of static computation will demand of them. The administration of *persons* will disappear for ever.

CHAPTER NINE

ECONOMIC CATEGORIES OF CAPITALISM
IN THE TRANSITION PERIOD[116]

1. Methodology of Marxist Economics: the Objectively-Social, Materially-Productive, and Historically-Dialectic Method. 2. Postulate of Equilibrium of the System of Production. 3. Modification of These Points of View During the Transition Period: Unproductive Acquisition of Use Values, Lack of Correct Reproduction, etc.; Lack of Equilibrium. 4. Commodity. 5. Value. 6. Price. 7. Wage and Profit. 8. "Naturalization"of Economic Thinking.

In the examination of the economics of the transformation period, one must not only deal with "pure" forms and categories. This examination is difficult because there are no stationary quantities present. If science in general in

* As Bukharin mentions in the footnote (#116), the co-author of this chapter, which comprises the most fundamental theoretical exercise of Marxist philosophical-economic thinking in this book, was Georg L. Pyatakov with whom he was closely connected from early youth until Bukharin joined Stalin in the fight against Trotskyism. Pyatakov and Bukharin—except Molotov, they were the two youngest of all Soviet leaders—belonged to the pre-1917 Bolshevik circle around the periodical "Kommunist," which was published in Stockholm by the three best known women in the movement: Aleksandra Kollontai, Ludmilla-Stahl and Eugenie Bosch. This circle constituted the "leftist" opposition to Lenin in such important problems of Bolshevism, as Anarchism, Peace of Brest-Litovsk, Trade-Unionism and the National Question. Although the arguments were often very vehement, Lenin treated this "fraction" within the Bolshevik party with special benevolence, and basically the same high respect he gave to Bukharin as theoretician of the party, Lenin extends in his "Testament" to Pyatakov.

its present condition does research into flowing "processes" and not fixed metaphysical "essences," then in the very period of transition the categories of being must for obvious reasons be replaced by categories of becoming. Fluidity, changeability, movement,—these traits are characteristic to a much greater degree of the transition period than of "normally" developing relations within the stable system of production. Therefore the question arises: are those methods and categories of thinking which Marx applied in relation to capitalist society, valid or invalid; are they valid now at the time of the breakdown of capitalism and the laying of the foundation of a new society?

To be sure. "In the analysis of economic forms, neither the microscope nor chemical reagents are of use. The force of abstraction must replace both."[117] By using the force of abstraction in researching the capitalist form of economy, Marx created an entire system of concepts, a system of tools of the knowledge of living economic reality. Not only in the hands of a genius, but also in the hands of all succeeding scientists—not the apologists and sycophants, but the really scientific investigators of the phenomena of economic life—these concepts constituted the basic means to the scientific comprehension of the economic process. To scientifically comprehend the economic process, one must understand it in its development, comprehend every phenomenon in its origin, its evolution, and its disappearance, and understand, as part of the whole, by what kind of scientific understanding the concepts defined by Marx operated without "failing." The cornerstone of the entire structure of the theoretical study of economy, i.e. the theory of the economy in its capitalist form,—the basic concepts of the entire system, were the concepts *commodity, value, price.*

134

But the knell of capitalist private property has sounded. The expropriators are expropriated. Capitalist production, with the inevitability of a natural law, arrived at a negation of itself. Communist revolution shakes the entire economic system to its foundations and smashes heretically the "time-honored" temple of capitalism. It begins a process of gigantic economic displacements and grandiose changes, a process of the restructuring of the entire system of production relations. The old interweaves with the new, the new struggles against the old, soon conquers it, soon recedes powerless. We must understand this complicated process in reference to a theory of knowledge, and will even here have to take refuge again and again in the force of abstraction.[118]

Already in the first serious attempt to scientifically comprehend that highly restless concrete, which we designate as the economy of the transition period, we hit upon the fact that the old concepts of theoretical economics fail in a flash. We hit upon a curious contradiction. The old categories of political economy remain as always forms of practical generalization of the continually changing, living economic reality. At the same time, however, these categories provide no possibility of penetrating beyond "the surface of phenomena," i.e. of freeing ourselves of vulgar thinking, of understanding the process of economic life in its totality and in its development. This is understandable. Those elementary relationships, the ideological expression of which is constituted by the categories of commodity, price, wage, profit, etc., exist in reality, and at the same time do not exist. They do not exist, and yet in a certain way they do exist; they exist as if they did not exist. They gain a strange ghostly-real and at the same time real-ghostly existence, somewhat like the souls of the deceased in the

135

Ancient Slavic mythology or like the pagan gods of the pious Christian Church. Therefore, the old proven tools of Marxist thinking, which were coined by Marx because of the real existence of corresponding relations of production, begin to easily fail. But in practical every-day use, they are still handled uncritically as a means to the real comprehension of the phenomena of economic life.[119]

The theoretical application of these categories presupposes now the complete comprehension of the narrowly historical character, the comprehension of the limits of their significance, the comprehension of the conditions, the meaning and the limits of their application to economic relations which are (in the process of) jumping across to tracks different in principle. Thus our job is to first analyze the starting points, the "methodology," of theoretical economics and to establish the role of its basic concepts; second, to pursue those modifications and limitations which arise for it in the system of the transition economy.

One can distinguish three character traits of Marxist economic methodology: the objectively social point of view, the point of view of material production, and finally the dialectically historical formulation of the question.

The *objectively social point of view* maintains the primacy of the society over the individual economic subject, the individual person. It considers the latter not as an "atom," not as isolated Robinson, but as a little part of the social system. "Production by isolated individuals outside of society . . . is as great an absurdity as the idea of the development of language without individuals living *together* and talking to one another."[120]

The *point of view* of material production maintains the primacy of production over consumption and over the entire economic life in general. The first (objective social)

L 112

136

point of view, which, as the mathematicians say, is a necessary one, is by no means sufficient for the characterization of the entire method. Society exists as a certain stable system. What are the material conditions for the existence of this system? "Every child knows that a country which ceased to work, I will not say for a year, but for a few weeks, would die.[121] The existence of society is determined by its production, which has a "socially specific character." Society itself is above all considered a "production organism," and the economy a "production process." The dynamic of production also determines the dynamic of needs. Production as a basic condition for the existence of society is a *given* element.[122]

The *dialectically historical method* observes society in its specifically historical forms and the general laws of social development in their concrete manifestation as laws of a specific social formation, which are limited in their operation by the historical limits of this formation.[123] Therefore economic categories, too, are "theoretical expressions of historical relations of production, corresponding to a specific level of development of material production."[124] Under no circumstances can they bear an eternal character as maintained by bourgeois science, which immortalizes them because it immortalizes the capitalist mode of production.[125]

L 113

Aside from this basic characteristic of the Marxist method, another methodological method must be emphasized which one can label as a *postulate of equilibrium*. We must treat this method especially thoroughly in consideration of its exceptional importance on the one hand, and its misunderstanding in the customary representations of Marxist teaching on the other hand.

In order to theoretically explain the capitalist system

137

of production relations, Marx proceeded from the *fact of their existence*. Once this system exists, social needs are satisfied—whether well or poorly—at least to such a degree that people not only do not die out, but live, work, and reproduce. In a society with social division of labor— and capitalist commodity society presupposes the latter— this means that a specific *equilibrium* of the entire system must be present. In necessary amounts one produces coal, iron, machines, cotton, linen, bread, sugar, boots, etc. In necessary amounts, the corresponding amount of living human labor will be applied to the production of all this. Here there may appear all kinds of deviations and fluctuations; the entire system expands, complicates itself, and develops, finds itself in constant motion and fluctuation, but on the whole persists in a condition of equilibrium.[126]

The discovery of this law of equilibrium constitutes the basic problem of theoretical economics. The result of the observation of the entire capitalist system *under the condition of its equilibrium* signifies theoretical economics as a scientific system.

"Every child "knows that the mass of products corresponding to the different needs require different and quantitatively determined masses of the total labour of society. That this necessity of distributing social labour in definite proportions cannot be done away with by the particular form of social production, but can only change the form it assumes, is *self evident*. . . . And the form in which this proportional division of labour operates, in a state of society where the interconnection of social labour is manifested in the private exchange of the individual products of labour, is precisely the exchange value of these products."[127]

Thus, short and to the point, here is expressed the solution to the basic problem, the problem of *value*.

138

If we consider the entire construction of "capital" from this point of view, then we see that the analysis begins with the firm, stable system of equilibrium. After a while, more complicated moments are inserted. The system falls into vacillation, becomes flexible. These vacillations do not lose their legitimate character, however, and the system as a whole is preserved, notwithstanding the most severe disturbances of equilibrium (crises). Through the disturbance of equilibrium appears a new equilibrium, of a higher order, so to speak. Only after one has recognized the laws of equilibrium can one go further and raise the question of the vacillations of the system. The crises themselves are considered not as an elimination of the equilibrium but as its disturbance; thereby Marx considers it necessary to discover and comprehend the law of this movement, not only how the equilibrium is disturbed but also how it is re-established. The crisis does not surpass the limits of the *vacillation* of the system. At the end of the observation we see *this system* move, vacillate; but throughout all movements and vacillations of equilibrium, it is always re-established again. The law of value is the law of equilibrium of the simple commodity system of production. The law of the costs of production is the law of equilibrium of the modified commodity system, the capitalist system. The law of market prices is the law of the vacillations of this system. The law of competition is the law of the constant re-establishment of the disturbed equilibrium. The law of crises is the law of the necessary periodic disturbance of equilibrium of the system and its re-establishment.

Marx formulated the question thus: the equilibrium is given—how is it possible? The equilibrium is disturbed—how is it re-established again? That is the *postulate of equilibrium*, the observation of the entire system in that *typical*

139

case, where the *question of the possibility of the non-re-establishment of equilibrium and the possibility of a decline of the system is not raised.*[128]

The observation of the social and thereby irrational, blind system from the point of view of equilibrium has, of course, nothing in common with the *harmonia praestabili-tata,* for the observation starts with the *fact* of the existence of this system and the *fact* of its development. The latter attributes to the model of this equilibrium *mobile* and not static equilibrium.

L 116

Those are the foundations of the methodology of theoretical economics. We must now move to the question of what meaning this point of view has in relation to the *period of the decay of capitalism and the period of the rule of the proletariat.*

The *socially objective* method remains obligatory and needs no limitations. In actuality, even in the process of social transformation, the subject depends upon the social milieu for its motives and its actions, even insofar as it remains as individual commodity producer. The task consists in analyzing the rebuilding of the *social* system. Here: (a) the collective, consciously economically active total subject—the proletarian state with all its coordinated organs—grows; (b) insofar as the anarchic commodity system is maintained, the irrational, blind "fate" of the market is maintained, i.e. again the *social* element, which increasingly comes under the regulating effect of the socially conscious center, which is being crystallized; (c) finally, insofar as the elements of the decay of social formations (e.g., the formation of closed, natural-economic cells) are present, they are on the one hand "limited" in their effects by the economic milieu (even their internal restructuring is a function of social displacements); on the other hand

L 117

L 118

140

they are pulled into the building process to a steadily increasing degree, by continually succumbing to the systematic influence on the part of the state-economic organization of the proletariat (compulsory labor, all sorts of taxes in kind). In this way it happens that even when individual elements fall out of the social production process, they find themselves within the constant sphere of influence of, and are even considered from the point of view of, the *social* system of production; in moments of their greatest remoteness they are theoretically interesting as an object of social attraction, as a potential component part of the new social system. | L 119

However, notwithstanding that the validity of the objectively social method remains, the latter gains an *altered logical tone*. In the examination of the social structure of capitalist commodity economy, all inherent laws bear the character of *elementary* laws, of a "blind" power, because the entire social process of production is irrational. Upon examining the structure of the transition period, the matter is different, for here occurs at an increasing rate a *rationalizing* of the social economic process. | L 120

The point of view of *material production* also remains valid on the whole. But it experiences essential changes and limitations. *First*, the production process itself is not an *a priori* given quantity. Stated more exactly: while in "normal" periods, social development of the process of social reproduction is given from the outset and an uninterrupted renewal of the elements of production is itself presupposed in the course of this production, the reproduction process in the transition period, in the convulsion of the entire social apparatus of labor, stands under the sign of uncertainty. Therefore, the problem here is not: "*how* is production possible?" but "*is* production possible?" One | L 121 can express the same thing from the point of view of productive powers: if in normal periods the development of productive powers constitutes the implicit pre-supposition of all theoretical observations, then here the question arises as to the possibility of their stationary condition as well as to the possibility of their catastrophic decline.

Second, an exceptionally strong decline and in places *suspension* of the process of production can appear. As long as the society does not die out, this is compensated for in another way: (a) by a frugal distribution of the leftovers of previous (purely capitalist) cycles of production,—here the process of consumption separates from the process of production and becomes incommensurate with it; (b) by L 122 the *forced* seizure of agricultural products from the village (here the differentiation from the "normal" situation is that this seizure is based only partly upon directly economic methods; consequently, only one half of the "national economy" takes part in the reproduction cycle); (c) by unproductive methods of acquisition of products (war booty, when the warehouses go from hand to hand, etc.).

Third, insofar as the production process is separate from the consumption process, insofar appear—even where the L 123 free market remains—the motives of consumption on the surface of the phenomena.

The *dialectical-historical method* succumbs not only to no limitations but, on the contrary, pushes itself into the foreground. The components of form of the new relationships, their fusion with the old ones, sometimes in highly remarkable combinations—all this makes a complex *sui generis* out of the production relations of the transition L 124 period. Furthermore, it is completely clear that the dialectic-historical point of view, which emphasizes the principle

142

of continual changeability of forms, the principle of the |
knowledge of *processes,* must inevitably be emphasized in |
the examination of the periods in which displacements of
social strata occur with the enormous speed of a sheer geo-
logical nature. The relative character of the "category" of
political economics is absolutely obvious.

The *postulate of equilibrium* is invalid. Equilibrium is to |L 125
be considered as a condition which the system must arrive
at (if it is to exist), but which it is unable to arrive at.
There is no proportionality between production and consumption or between the different branches of production.
(In parenthesis: also none between the subjective elements of the system.) Therefore it is fundamentally amiss
to try to apply the categories, the concepts and laws corresponding to the condition of equilibrium to the transition
period. One could reply that insofar as society has not
perished, an equilibrium exists. Such argumentation would
be correct if the section of time which we are consider-
ing represented a great duration. Outside of equilibrium, |L 126
society can not live *for long,* it dies. But this same social
system can persist for a while in "abnormal" conditions, i.e.
outside the condition of equilibrium. In this case a certain |L 127
relative equilibrium (insofar as we have no compensation |
outside of production, which in the long run is also impos-
sible) is bought at the price of a partial *destruction of the* |L 128
system itself.

In this way, the general character of changes and variations in the method of examination can be expressed as
follows: in the analysis of the transition period a whole
series of methodological simplifications is inadmissible,
which under conditions of a stable production system are
entirely admissible and appropriate. *Marx* formulated the

question as follows: how is the existence of a given economic form possible and what are the laws of its origin, its development, and its disappearance?

The *revised* formulation for the transition period runs: what are the material conditions for the existence of society at the given moment, how long can they exist under the given conditions; how is production possible; is the establishment of an equilibrium possible; what result would appear in the case of equilibrium and what result in a negative reply to this question; what is the alteration of production relations in *both* cases, what are the laws of movement in *both* cases, etc.?

Now we have to move to certain basic concepts of political economics, in order to determine the degree of their application to the period under consideration. For "these ideas, these categories, are as little eternal as the relations L 129 they express. They are historical and transitory products."[129]

The limits of the applicability of these categories become clear at once when we determine the basic conditions for the existence of the real changing relations which correspond to them (the categories).

Commodity. This category assumes above all a *social division of labor or a splintering of labor* and the resulting *failure of a conscious regulator* of the economic processes. In differentiation to the use values of commodities, social division of labor is revealed; in its value is revealed the general connection of labor between the parts of the system which has no conscious regulator. In order for any product or simply an object to become a commodity, a condition of stable social ties is not indispensably necessary. Thus, for example, the so-called "accidental" arrangements. Often the social connections are set here for the first time (overseas merchants in rare expeditions, rare colonial commodities, etc.).[130] In all these cases, however, the commodity cannot be a universal form. Commodity production and commodity economy as a model of social structure is missing here; even a unified economy cannot be anything (e.g., the earlier colonial exchange). The commodity can only be a universal category insofar as a continual and not accidental social connection is present on an *anarchist base of production.* Consequently, *insofar as in place of the elementary power, a conscious social regulator appears, the commodity is transformed into product and loses its commodity character.*

| L 130
| L 131

The value emerges when we have regular *commodity production.* Not the accidental but the constant model of anarchic connection through exchange is mandatory. Here, too, a condition of *equilibrium* is necessary. The law of value is no more than the law of equilibrium in the anarchic commodity system. From this point of view it is clear, for example, that the exchange of ivory for coral (there, where, as Marx said, the exchange is really a deceit) is not a value exchange. Not every exchange is a *commodity* exchange (when little boys exchange feathers or when the proletarian state practices the *exchange of products* between city and country). On the other hand, not every commodity exchange is a *value* exchange (e.g. the exchange on the "free market" with its preposterous prices is not a value exchange, even though it is a commodity exchange). *Consequently, value as a category of the capitalist commodity system in its equilibrium is the least useful for the transition period where commodity production disappears to a major degree and where equilibrium is absent.*

| L 132

| L 133

The *price* is, generally stated, an expression of the value

145

relation. But not always. In the first case, one can distinguish the following variations: (a) value agrees with the price of the quantity (static equilibrium of the simple commodity system); (b) value does not agree with the quantity (typical case); (c) the price is a derived amount, adapted to the commodity, which as such has no value (e.g., value of landed property, as capitalized rent). From these cases the *appearance*-form must be differentiated, where the price is not based on a value relation. The price is totally detached from the value. *In the transition period, therefore, the case of the appearance-form inevitably approaches the typical case.*

This phenomenon is for its part also tied to the collapse of the *money system*. Money represents that real social tie, those knots, in which the entire developed *commodity system* of production is entangled. It is conceivable that in the transition period, in the process of the annihilation of the commodity system as such, a process of "self-negation" of money occurs. It is expressed at first in so-called "money devaluation," second, in the fact that the distribution of money symbols becomes dependent on the distribution of products, and vice versa. Money ceases to be a universal equivalent and becomes a conventional—and thereby highly imperfect—symbol of the circulation of products.

Wages become an illusory quantity which have no content. As long as the working class is the ruling class, *wage labor* disappears. In socialized production there is *no* wage labor. And insofar as there is no wage labor, there are also *no wages* as the price of the labor power sold to the *capitalists*. Only the outer shell remains of wages—the money form, which together with the money system approaches self-annihilation. *In the system of the proletarian*

146

dictatorship, the "worker" receives a social share (in Russian, *"payok"*), *but no wages.*　L 134

Likewise, the category of *profit* as well as *the category of surplus value*, insofar as we speak of new production cycles, disappears. However, to the extent that the "free market" still exists, that usurers and the black market trade exist, speculative profit is also present, although its laws of motion are determined differently than in the normal capitalist system. The monopolistic situation of the buyer plays a role here, because it lets him absorb quantities of products from other spheres.　L 135

Stated generally, one of the basic tendencies of the transition period is the *rending of the veils of commodity fetishism*. Together with the growing natural system of economic relations of society, the corresponding ideological categories are also exploded. And once this is the case, the necessity arises out of the theory of the economic process to pass on to natural scientific thinking, i.e. to observation of society and its parts as systems of elements in their natural form.

CHAPTER TEN

THE "EXTRA-ECONOMIC" COMPULSION
IN THE TRANSITION PERIOD

*1. Force and Compulsion in their Relation to Economics.
2. Use of Force in the Transition Periods. 3. State Power
as Concentrated Use of Force. 4. Economic Meaning of
Proletarian Dictatorship. 5. Force and Compulsion in
Relation to Non-Proletarian Groups. 6. Compulsion as
the Expression of the Self-Organization of the Working
People. 7. The Dying Out of Compulsion.*

In theoretical political economy, i.e. in the science which
researches the elementary laws of capitalist commodity
economy, "purely economic" categories dominate. "In actual history it is notorious that conquest, enslavement, robbery, murder, briefly force, play a great part. In the
tender annals of Political Economy, the idyllic reigns from
time immemorial. Right and 'labour' were from all time
the sole means of enrichment, the present year of course
always excepted."[131] It is beyond a doubt that in the entire
course of the historical process, the role of force and of
compulsion was extraordinarily great. In this soil, especially, theories were able to sprout which see in force the

alpha and omega of history.[132] On the other hand, a whole series of opposed theories are based on the negation of force, which simply do not want to see the phenomena provided by experience—all those facts which stubbornly demand an explanation. Marxism cannot think away that which is really there as the greatest historical factor. The plundering of the community estates in England in the period of primitive accumulation, the forced labor of the slave masses in old Egypt, the colonial wars, the "great uprisings" and "glorious revolutions," imperialism, the communist revolution of the proletariat, the workers army in the Soviet Republic—are not all these phenomena, so different in kind, bound up with the question of compulsion? Of course. The vulgar researcher wants to reassure himself by reconciling all contradictory opinions. The follower of the dialectical method must analyze these forms in their connection to the whole, in their specific properties, in their—sometimes totally opposed in essence—functional meaning.

The social use of force and compulsion (and here we speak only of this) has a two-fold relation to economics: first, it arises as a function of this economics; second, on its part it influences economic life. In this latter role, the influence can be exerted in two directions: either in the line of economic relationships which are developing objectively,—then it satisfies the social need which has become mature, *accelerates* economic development, constitutes a progressive form of this development; or it stands in opposition to this development,—then it *delays* the development, forms its "chains," and must in general make room for another form of compulsion with another, if one may so express it, mathematical sign.[133] Especially plastically does the role of

149

force reveal itself in the "critical epochs." "Wars and revolutions are the locomotives of history." And these two "locomotives" represent forms—and thereby the most sharply expressed forms—of force. Marx wrote about the transition from feudalism to capitalism: "These methods depend in part on brute force, e.g., the colonial system. But they all employ the power of the State, the concentrated and organized force of society, to hasten hothouse fashion, the process of transformation of the feudal mode of production into the capitalist mode, and to shorten the transition. Force is the midwife of every old society pregnant with a new one. It is itself an economic power."[134]

L 136

L 137

In the transition period, where one production structure is succeeded by another, the obstetrician is the revolutionary force. This revolutionary force must break the chains of the development of society, i.e. on the one hand the old forms of "concentrated force," which have become a counterrevolutionary factor, the old state and the old model of production relations. On the other hand, this revolutionary force must actively promote the formation of new production relations, while it creates a new form of "concentrated force," the state of new classes, which force operates as a lever of economic revolution, and changes the economic structure of society.[135] On the one hand, therefore, force plays the role of a destructive factor; on the other hand, it is the power of cohesion, of organization, of building. The greater this "extra-economic" power, which in reality represents an "economic exponent," the smaller are the "expenses" of the transition period (of course, all conditions otherwise being equal), the *shorter* is this transition period, the faster appears a social equilibrium on a new base, and the quicker the curve of produc-

150

tive powers begins to rise. This exponent is not some kind of super-empirical, mystical quantity: it is the power of the class which carries out the revolution, its social power. It is therefore completely clear that its magnitude is dependent above all upon the degree of organization of this class. And the revolutionary class is the most organized when it has constituted itself as state power. For this reason, state power constitutes the "concentrated and organized force of society." For this reason, *revolutionary* state power is the mightiest lever of economic revolution. | L 138

In the period of transition from capitalism to communism, the revolutionary class, the creator of the new society, is the proletariat. Its state power, its dictatorship, the soviet state, constitutes a factor of the destruction of old economic connections and the creation of new ones. "Political power in the actual sense is merely the organized power of one class for oppressing another."[136] As far as this political might as "concentrated force" over the bourgeoisie itself represents an *economic* power, it is a power which explodes capitalist production relations, places the materially objective skeleton of production at the disposal of the proletariat, and gradually introduces *nonproletarian* subjective elements of production into the system of new social production connections. On the other hand, however, this "concentrated force" turns *inward,* by constituting a factor of the *self-organization and the compulsory self-discipline of the working people.* We must therefore examine both sides of coercion: in relation to nonproletarian groups and in relation to the proletariat itself and to the social groups standing close to it. | L 139 | L 140 | L 141

The ruling proletariat has against it in the first phase of its domination: (1.) the parasitic groups (former estate owners, all kinds of rentiers, bourgeois producers, who have little relationship to the production process, merchant capitalists, speculators, stock-exchange speculators, bankers); (2.) the unproductive administrative aristocracy recruited from these groups (higher bureaucrats of the capitalist state, generals, bishops, etc.); (3.) bourgeois producers as organizers and managers (organizers of trusts and syndicates, businessmen of the industrial world, big engineers, who are directly tied in with the capitalist world, inventors, etc.); (4.) the qualified bureaucracy in civil, military, and clerical positions; (5.) the technical mental laborers and mental laborers in general (engineers, technicians, agronomists, doctors, professors, lawyers, journalists, most teachers, etc.); (6.) the officers; (7.) the wealthy large-scale farmers; (8.) the urban middle class and partially the petit bourgeoisie in the cities; (9.) the clergy, including the unqualified clergy.

L 142 | All these strata, classes, and groups inevitably wage an active struggle against the proletariat under the political leadership of the representatives of finance capital and the military leadership of the generals. These attacks must be repelled, the enemy must be disorganized. It is necessary to suppress its other methods of struggle (sabotage), etc. All this can only bring about the "concentrated force." To the

L 143 | extent that the proletariat is victorious in this struggle and that its forces gather themselves more and more around the basic crystallization point of social revolutionary energy—i.e. the dictatorship of the proletariat—there begins an accelerated process of disintegration of the old ways of thinking on the part of the economically useful and non-parasitic groups in the enemy camp. These elements must

L 144 | be taken into consideration, gathered, placed in a new position, fitted into the new framework of labor. And this can only happen with the support of the organization of the proletarian state, working with coercive measures. This organization accelerates the process of the acceptance of those subjective elements which are also useful in the new system,—above all, the technical mental laborers. It goes without saying that these powers, without the pressure of force, cannot be put to use systematically and with social expediency. For the old remnants of ideas which are still present in the heads of these categories of persons, with their partly individualistic, partly anti-proletarian patterns of thinking, conceive of the plan of social expediency as the most brutal encroachment upon the rights of the | L 145 "free personality." External state force is therefore here an absolute necessity. In the course of development, with a constant re-education of these strata, according to the extent | L 146 of their class deformation and their transformation into social laborers, the elements of force will keep diminishing. It is clear that the process of psychological re-education is that much more difficult and that much more painful the higher the corresponding group stood on the ladder of the capitalist hierarchy; social groups whose being is the most closely tied to the specific forms and methods of capitalist production submit with the most resistance to the social remodeling. The direct struggle with them in the first phase of the revolution, their transferal into such relations where they can perform socially useful labor without being able to damage the building of communism, the expedient distribution of these powers, the correct politics in relation to them, which changes according to their psychological capacity—all this implies, finally, a "sanctioning" of the "concentrated force," which watches over the genesis of the | L 147 communist society.

Compulsion does not limit itself, however, to the framework of the previously ruling classes and the groups which are near to them. In the transition period it is transferred—in altered forms—to the working people themselves, even to L 148 the ruling class. This side of the question must be examined more exactly.

L 149 In the transition period, one can not limit the analysis by presupposing a perfect unity of class. In investigating the abstract laws of the capitalist mechanism, it was not necessary that one remain with the molecular movements within the classes and the differentiation of these "real totalities." They were accepted as a quantity which is more or less unified. A translation of this view—which is completely correct in the framework of abstract theoretical analysis of "pure capitalism"—to the analysis of the transition period with its highly fluent forms, with its, so to speak, principal L 150 dynamic, would mean the most primitive methodological error. Not only the mechanics between the classes but also the mechanics within the classes must be taken into consideration. The changing relation of social powers as well as the relations within the classes are highly mobile quantities whose mobility in the "critical epochs" becomes especially great.[137]

While man influences nature, he also changes his own nature, said Marx. But the same also happens in the course of the social struggle. Herein exists the process of the revolutionary *education* of the proletariat. If one considers this process from the point of view of stratifications within L 151 the classes, one can call it a process of the constant approaching of the middle and lower strata of the working class to its avant-garde. The transformation of the "class in itself" into the "class for itself" is perfected. The view which the atoning nobleman[138] has of the "people" consists

154

of an idealization of every member of the lower class *in concreto*. The proletarian-Marxist point of view operates with really existing quantities.

The proletariat arrives at its domination as a class. But this in no way signifies a unified character of this class in which every member represents an ideal cross section. The proletarian vanguard actively leads the others. It is a purposeful, organizing force, operating deliberately. It | L 152 seizes hold of the sympathy of the middle stratum which instinctively "sympathizes" with the revolution but is not in a position to lucidly formulate the goals and to precisely prescribe the path. In the course of development, there is *no* line of demarcation between the avant-garde and this very large stratum. Just the opposite. Increasingly new powers are constantly being pulled into the front stratum. This process is that of internal welding together, which makes the class a class. Behind the middle class of sympathizers is the stratum of the indifferent ones; then come the so-called fellow travellers. The process of development, however, encompasses them too: the proletarian avant-garde grows, expands numerically, absorbs increasingly greater strata of classes, which keep becoming a "class for itself."

If we touch upon this question from a somewhat altered point, we will find, for example, such groupings: the core of the industrial proletariat, which has dissolved the bond with the rural population, of the typical working class, constantly employed in industry; the workers aristocracy, which is exceptionally tied to the interests of capital (the especially qualified workers of America, Germany, England; the printers in almost all countries, etc.); the seasonal workers who periodically enter the sphere of industry and

155

then leave it again; workers with appendages of private property (little houses, sometimes land, etc.); workers who are tied to the country, sometimes also working the land; workers who became workers in the war, who did not make it through capitalist schooling, sometimes recruited from the urban petit bourgeoisie, craftsmen, traders, etc.; workers who have been specifically isolated by the capitalist states according to a social political characteristic (e.g. certain strata of railroad workers); rural workers, servants, gang-men, etc. In this way one gets a fairly colorful picture of the "being" of the different categories of the working class and also of their social consciousness. It is evident that among these groups are also groups which have been completely corrupted by capitalism, with maximal narrow egotistical motives. But even relatively broad circles of the working class bear the stamp of the capitalist commodity world. From this results the necessity of *compulsory discipline,* the compulsory character of which is that much more tangible the less the internal voluntary discipline, i.e. the less revolutionary the given group or stratum of the proletariat is. Even the proletarian avant-garde which is united in the party of the revolution, in the communist party, introduces such *compulsory self-discipline* to its own ranks; it is scarcely felt by many components of this avant-garde since it agrees with the internal motives. But still it is there.[139] But it is not introduced by an alien power but expresses the collective will of all and is binding for everyone.

It is obvious that this element of compulsion, which is here the self-compulsion of the working class, grows from the crystallized center towards the significantly more amorphous and dispersed periphery. *This is the conscious power*

L 153

L 154

of cohesion of the little parts of the working class, which, power represents for some categories, subjectively, an external pressure, which constitutes for the entire working class, objectively, its accelerated self-organization.

In *communist* society there will be an absolute freedom of "personality," and any kind of external regulation of relationships between people will be absent; that is, self-activity without force will exist. In *capitalist* society there was no self-activity for the working class and only force *from the side of the enemy class.* In the *transition period* the self-activity of the working class is present along with the force which the working class, as a class for itself, introduces for all its parts. The contradiction between force and self-activity expresses the self-contradictory character of the transition period itself, since the proletariat has already abandoned the framework of capitalist compulsion, but has not *yet* become a member of communist society.

L 155

One of the main forms of compulsion of the new kind which operates in the sphere of the working class itself is the abolition of the so-called freedom to work. "Freedom to work" in capitalist society means one of the numerous fictions of this society, for in reality the monopolizing of the means of production by the capitalists *forces* the workers to sell their labor power. This "freedom" was based on the following: first, on a relative possibility of *choosing* one's master (moving from one factory to another), the possibility "of leaving" and of being "dismissed"; second, this "freedom" meant *competition among the workers themselves.* In this last sense, "freedom to work" was already partly conquered in the period of capitalism by the *workers organizations,* when unions partly eliminated competition between workers by uniting them, organizing the

157

splintered parts of the class, joining them, and making them stronger in their struggle against the capitalist class. The unions made the demand that only members of the unions be admitted to the factory; they declared a boycott (i.e. used force) against strikebreakers, this living incarnation of the bourgeois "freedom to work," etc. Under the dictatorship of the proletariat, the question of the "master" falls aside, since the "expropriators" are "expropriated." On the other hand, the remnants of disorganization, unsolidarity, individualism, guild restrictions, the depravity of capitalist society in not recognizing the *universal proletarian tasks*, which receive their concentrated expression in the tasks and demands of the soviet dictatorship, of the workers state. Since these tasks must be mastered at any price, it is understandable that from the point of view of the proletariat, in the very name of actual and non-fictitious freedom of the working class, an abolition of the so-called "freedom to work" is required. For the latter no longer agrees with the regularly organized "planned economy" and a corresponding distribution of labor powers. Consequently, the regime of compulsory labor and state distribution of labor powers in the dictatorship of the proletariat already expresses a relatively high degree of organization of the entire apparatus and the stability of proletarian power on the whole.[140]

In the capitalist regime, compulsion was defended in the name of the "interests of the totality," while it was in reality in the interests of capitalist groups. Under proletarian dictatorship, compulsion is for the first time really the tool of the majority in the interest of this majority.

L 156

The proletariat as class is the only class to which prejudices of possession are on the whole foreign. But the prole-

158

tariat must operate side by side with the often very large *peasantry*. If the large farmers actively struggle against the measures of the proletarian dictatorship, then the "concentrated force" of the proletariat must more or less offer resistance to the Vendée of the Kulaks. But the masses of middle and sometimes even poor peasantry vacillate constantly, new led by the hate of capitalist exploitation by the large-estate owners, a hate which drives them into the arms of communism, and now motivated by the feeling of being owner (and consequently in the period of famine also that of being a *black-market dealer*), which drives them into the army of the reaction. The latter is expressed in the resistance to the state monopoly of grain and in the struggle for free trade which is speculation, as well as for speculation which is free trade—in resistance to the system of compulsory labor and in general to any forms of state restraint of the economic anarchy. These stimuli appear especially when the exhausted cities can offer no equivalent in the first period for the grain and for the sacrifices to the "common pot." Therefore, compulsion constitutes an absolute and peremptory necessity.

L 157

L 158

L 159

Therefore: in relation to the previous *bourgeois groups,* compulsion from the side of the proletarian dictatorship is a compulsion from the side of another class which wages a class struggle against the object of its compulsion; in relation to the non-exploitative mass of farmers, compulsion from the side of the proletariat is a class struggle insofar as the farmer is owner and speculator; compulsion signifies union of the peasantry with the labor organization, education and attracting to the building of communism insofar as the farmer is a working man and non-exploiter, an enemy of capitalism; finally, in relation to the *proletariat* itself,

L 160

159

compulsion is a method of organization which is introduced by the working class itself, i.e. a method of forced, accelerated *self-organization*.

From a broader point of view, i.e. from the point of view of a historical scale of greater scope, proletarian compulsion in all its forms, from executions to compulsory labor, constitutes, as paradoxical as this may sound, a method of the formation of a new communist humanity from the human material of the capitalist epoch. In actuality, the epoch of proletarian dictatorship is at the same time an epoch of *class deformation*. Capitalism was followed by a more or less progressive social *splintering* of the society: it disintegrated the peasantry, annihilated the "middle class," and drove class contradictions to their extreme. The dictatorship of the proletariat, which in the first period expresses the crassest division of the capitalist world, *begins*, after the commencement of a certain equilibrium, *to re-collect humanity*. The previous bourgeoisie, which has now been conquered, struck, held down, and impoverished, learns physical labor, undergoes mental changes, and is re-educated. A part of the bourgeoisie is destroyed in the civil war, but that part which survives already represents another social category. Likewise, the intellectuals. The peasantry, which in the general stream maintains more position than the others, is nevertheless drawn into the universal channel, and slowly but surely experiences a transformation. The proletariat itself likewise changes its "own nature." In this way specific class distinctions are blurred; the classes begin to decay as classes and to become like the proletariat. A period of class *deformation* begins. The lever of this deformation is the proletarian dictatorship. As concentrated application of force, the dictatorship finally abolishes any kind of force. As the highest expression of the class, it

L 161

L 162

160

abolishes all classes. As regime of the class which has organized itself as state power, it prepares the extinction of every state. By carrying on the struggle for its existence, it annihilates its own existence. In classless, state-less, communist society, where in place of discipline from without, the simple joy of working on the part of the normal social human being will have appeared, the external norms of human behavior will lose all meaning. Compulsion, no matter what its form, will disappear once and for all.

L 162 a

CHAPTER ELEVEN

THE PROCESS OF WORLD REVOLUTION AND
THE WORLD SYSTEM OF COMMUNISM

*1. The System of Equilibrium of the World Economy.
2. War as Disturbance of the Equilibrium of Production.
3. Collapse of the System, Starting with the Weaker Links.
4. Models of Communist Revolution. 5. The Interchanging
Relation between the Proletarian State and the Bourgeois
State. 6. Communist Revolution and Capitalist Colonies.
7. Crystallization of the Soviet Republics and their Alli-
ances. 8. Proletarian World Dictatorship and its Abolition.
9. The World System of Communism.*

Before the war, the system of world economy found itself in a condition of mobile equilibrium. The exchange
process between countries, the international movement of
capital (capital export and import), the international displacement of labor powers bound the individual parts of
this system with firm ties of "normal" processes, which are
vital for the existence of the world economy itself and its
component elements. The laws of the capitalist commodity
system which were analyzed in their abstract form from
pure theory as laws of abstract, "pure" capitalist society

162

and were realized in the epoch of industrial capital concretely in the framework of territories marked off as states, became, above all, elementary laws of the anarchic *world* system. World prices and consequently also social world labor as their regulator "in the last instance"; world competition; the world market; the tendency of the rate of interest towards a unified world average; the balancing of wages and their tendency towards a world balance which moved labor power from one country into the other; the crises, etc.; and similar things,—all this was the expression of the basic *fact* of the system of *world* capitalism, which found itself in a condition of mobile equilibrium, but which developed in contradictions.

This universal relatedness and mutual dependency of individual capitalist states, the circumstance that they | L 163
were components of the total system, resulted inevitably in the *international* character of the war. Just as the crises, as a very consequence of the strength of the relation between the parts of the world economy, had taken on the character of *world* crises, the war had to assume the character of an enormous world slaughter. The crisis expands and rolls on in waves, because the disturbance of equilibrium in one part of the system inevitably carries over into all its parts like on a telegraph wire. Under the conditions of world economy the war, which signifies a disturbance of | L 164
equilibrium in one place, transforms itself with natural necessity into an enormous shock of the entire system, into a world war. The breaking of the ties of world economy signifies its decay into pieces, and the process of expanded negative reproduction, which was carried out as a result of this rupture within the countries waging war, led at last to the collapse of the entire system.

With which links did this collapse have to begin? It is

163

self-evident that it had to begin with those links which were weakest in an *organizational capitalist* respect.[141]

In actuality, we already saw in Chapter 3 of this work that the stability of private capitalist systems within the world economy, as far as the war became a concrete fact, found their explanation in that internal reorganization of production relations which led to the form of state capitalism. On the whole one can therefore say that the stability

L 165 | of these systems was directly proportional to the level of state capitalist organization. Without this, capitalism could not even live through the span of time which history has cleared for it. This stability, tied to the form of state capitalism, was to be seen at the level of production as well as at the level of the social classes. However, the state capi-

L 166 | talist form of national economy was itself only possible upon a specific "maturity" of capitalist relations in general. It was that much more perfect the greater—under otherwise identical conditions—the development of productive powers, the greater the finance capitalist organization, the

L 167 | greater the totality of monopolistic relationships of modern capitalism. It was that much less perfect the more backward and agrarian the respective country was, the less developed its productive powers were, the weaker the finance capitalist organization of its economy was. But not only from the point of view of the economic and social struc-

L 168 | ture but also from the technological-productive point of view, the systems with the highest level of technology had to prove to be the most stable in the gigantic conflict,—the technology which the imperialist war demanded. This *technology* was of decisive military significance. The perfection of the *form of organization* compensated in part for the process of expanded negative reproduction. The *concentration of the social strength* of the bourgeoisie in

164

state power, which had intergrown with the economic organizations of capital, created an enormous resistance to the workers movement. Therefore, the collapse of the capitalist world system began with the weakest systems in terms of political economy, with the least developed state capitalist organizations.[142] | L 169

One must by no means confuse the question of the level of the model of revolution under consideration with the question of the chronological sequence of proletarian revolutions. The level of the model of revolution is determined by the specific weight of that complex of production relations which are incorporated in the proletariat. The greater the relative extent of concentration of the proletariat, the higher is the model of communist revolution, the more difficult it is to be *victorious*, but the easier it is to *build*.[143] The organizational preconditions of communism lie, as we have seen, in the area of concentrated means of production and socialized labor. In the capitalist world system, these preconditions find their particularly crass expression in the "superpowers" of capital, where the power of the bourgeoisie is especially strong. But for that very reason, because we are dealing with an anarchic world system, with a special situation of "world economy," the possibility of exploitation of the colonies has, on the other hand, been created for the "great" imperialist systems. And from this soil arises another possibility, namely the possibility of a transitional "community of interests" between the imperialist "fatherland" and the working class. This "community of interests," for its part, has enormously inhibited the | L 170 course of the revolution, which is based on the cessation of every mutuality between bourgeoisie and proletariat. And nevertheless, insofar as the revolution is a given fact, it is in its model the highest in those very countries where

165

the working class makes up the largest percentage of the entire population and where the means of production are concentrated the most strongly. For with these two factors are given first, the material-objective skeleton of the new society and second, its basic production relations. From this point of view it becomes completely clear why the revolution of the proletariat was first carried out in Russia. Here the state machinery was organized the most weakly. The forms of state capitalism were only in the process of being formed. The technological weakness of the country, which was on the whole agrarian, determined an unheard-of military debacle. The state apparatus proved to be so unstable that it could be relatively easily overthrown by the proletriat in the large urban centers. But, on the other hand, the

L 171 causes of the easy victory are dialectically transformed after the victory of the proletariat into causes of the greatest difficulties. The economic backwardness of the country, the great field of riven, splintered labor of small owners in contrast to really socialized labor,—all this presents enormous obstacles for the organizing of a systematic structure of social economy. The revolution had been easily victorious because the proletariat, which strove for communism, was supported by the peasantry, which marched against the estate owners. But the same peasantry proves to be the greatest brake in the period of the building of communist production relations.

On the other hand, in Germany the revolution proceeds much more painfully. The capitalist state puts up a much more stubborn resistance; the proletariat represents the only revolutionary power; the victory is difficult to achieve. But the model of the revolution is on a higher level, although the revolution comes later.[144]

If we consider the revolutionary process on its world

166

scale, therefore, we can set up the following universal principles: *the process of world revolution begins with the partial systems of the world economy which have a lower niveau where the victory of the proletariat is easier but the crystallization of new relationships is more difficult; the speed of the assault of the revolution is in inverse proportion to the maturity of capitalist relationships and the level of the model of revolution.*

L 172

The end of imperialist war is not able to bring to a halt the decay of the capitalist system, its collapse, the communist revolution of the proletariat. The sinking of productive power continues even after the peace treaty. The imperialists believed they could organize the world economy with methods which negate world economy. The victors believed they could pull themselves out of their awkward situation by merciless exploitation, which finally eliminates every possibility of this exploitation. But the spirit of world competition plays them a dirty trick and forces them to fight each other. Thus history shows imperialism its fateful *a posteriori*, which impetuously offers itself to the "victors" in its total frightful nakedness.[145]

The economic isolation and the severance of relations during the war, the results of this condition after the war, intensify the process of destruction of productive powers and accelerate the collapse of the capitalist system, link for link; the revolutionary takeover of power by the proletariat and the revolution in the mode of production, even if it is only in one country, extraordinarily intensify the destruction of the old ideology, "revolutionize" the working class in the other countries, the presupposition of which has already been given by the entire preceding development. In the first Soviet Republics, the proletariat has its organizations which dispose of a maximum of social and

167

material power. In the middle of the decaying world system of capitalist economy they therefore inevitably build new crystallization points, centers for attracting proletarian energy and the greatest factor for further decomposition of the capitalist system. In the entire capitalist world the shock advances, regardless of attempts to breathe new life into capitalism, with giant steps forward. Productive powers sink. Production relations fall into disintegration and decay. The economic equilibrium between spheres of production is missing, and the disturbance of equilibrium assumes increasingly primitive forms. The social class equilibrium is also missing, and it comes to decisive conflict. The political organization or, more correctly, the states of the bourgeoisie experience a crisis, for world imperialism proves itself incapable of carrying out an absolutely unified policy, equal in all its parts. The capitalist armies disintegrate. As long as the production anarchy of the world and its expression, world competition, dictate to the bourgeois state organizations their blind wills, the entire process increasingly assumes the elementary character of decay. The elementary nature of capitalist relationships creates on the base of its destruction that characteristic condition of insecurity which proclaims the near end. And in the middle of this dissolving web of capitalist economy, *growing* organizations of a new model emerge, in which the possibility of *development* has been principally provided, for only here is a restoration of social equilibrium possible; organizations, which out of the very disintegration of the capitalist systems obtain the excess amount of their own power: the proletarian states with a new system of economic relations which stabilize themselves that much more, the weaker the old decaying capitalist groupings become. The capitalist world order of the epoch of industrial capital

L 173

168

was the incorporation of an elementary process, for there reigned a total lack of regulation of relationships; the role of the conscious regulator was played by the unconscious "market." The state capitalist form of society, which had left world relationships unorganized, replaced unconscious processes with the conscious regulation of economic relationships by putting the class program of the bourgeoisie in place of the elementary laws of the commodity economy. The epoch of the decay of state capitalist organizations enchains anew this elementary power, which is differentiated from the commodity-elementary power of the past by the direction of its movement: there the elementary power was the lever of capitalist concentration and centralization, the *growth* of capitalist society and finally its organization; here this elementary power constitutes the lever of the decay of the organizational system into parts. And again: in the middle of this elementary process of decay, a process of organization and rationalization of economic life can only exist in the proletarian states, but already on a principally different base. The decomposition and decay of the old system and the organization of the new are the *most basic* and most universal laws of the transition period. Whatever the deviations may be, the results proceed in the direction of socialism. The relation between proletarian states and bourgeois states can best be seen in their war-like clashes, in class war, where the old armies decompose, because in the whole course of development, a social equilibrium on a capitalist base has become impossible. | L 174

The most important factor in the decay of the capitalist system is the dissolution of the relations between imperialist states and their numerous colonies. The so-called "national state" even in the prewar period was the purest fic- | L 175

L 175 tion. In reality, there existed subjects of colonial policy, imperialist states, which represented complicated systems with a stable nucleus and a coordinated periphery, and subjects of this colonial policy with different shadings and levels of coordination. In the very formation of these gigantic bodies, the organized "extra-economic" force, which, as Marx said, is itself an economic force, played an enormous role. "Power politics," "army and fleet," and the other stimuli of imperialism were means of organization of the imperialist state systems. The state tie, which in the last analysis was based on armed might, was of decisive significance.

L 176 To the extent that the state power of capital disintegrated, a disintegration of the imperialist systems had to begin, a decrease of colonies, a splintering of the "superpowers," the elimination of independent "national states." From the point of view of the struggle of social powers, this can express itself in a series of colonial uprisings, national uprisings, small national wars, etc. Certainly, the colonial uprisings and the national revolutions (Ireland, India, China, etc.) have absolutely no *direct* relationship to the developing proletarian revolution; their *local* and direct significance in no way consists of the introduction of the dictatorship of the proletariat; the proletariat does not play the leading political role here, for it is extremely weak. But nevertheless, these colonial uprisings and national revolutions form a component part of the great revolu-

L 177 tionary world process, which shifts the entire axis of world economy. For objectively, factors have been given for the universal decay of capitalist production relations, a decay which facilitates the victory of the proletarian revolution and the dictatorship of the working class.

The dictatorship of the proletariat can not be victorious if the proletariat of different countries is isolated from each other. Therefore a union, a cohesion, a welding together, an alliance between all arising proletarian soviet republics is already indispensably necessary in the course of the struggle. Even for the bourgeoisie, a world alliance in the transition period is objectively necessary: necessary even in respect to economics, for only in this way can they hope to overcome the crisis; the alliance is also necessary for them in respect to politics, for only then can they resist the proletariat: thus the attempts to create a "League of Nations." However, the decay of the capitalist system which has already begun, its enormous disorganization, and the quantity of newly arisen frictions exceptionally intensify the decentralization tendencies, and thus the bourgeoisie experiences a shipwreck. The element of decay stifles the organizational reason of the bourgeoisie. For the *proletariat,* its economic and political unity is a matter of life or death. And since its partial victories (its dictatorship) signify an overcoming of the decay, there results from this the objective necessity of the consolidation of the proletarian state system. To the extent that the economic and political web of the world economy is restructured and the emphasis transferred to the proletarian states and their alliance, the entire picture of the world economy is changed. The previous colonies and the backwards agrarian countries, where no proletarian dictatorship exists, nevertheless enter into an economic affiliation with the socialist industrial republics. They are gradually pulled into the socialist system, according to somewhat the same model along which the rural agriculture of the individual socialist countries is pulled in.

Thus the world dictatorship of the proletariat gradually grows. With its growth, the resistance of the bourgeoisie recedes, and the complexes of bourgeoisie which were left

L 178

171

over at the end will probably acquiesce with all their organizations *in corpore*.[146]

But the world dictatorship of the proletariat signifies
basically the beginning of the negation of the dictatorship
of the proletariat in general. The state power of the working
class necessarily grows as long as the resistance of the capitalist groups grows. Since the process of the development
of capitalist collapse and communist revolution signifies a
complete historical stage, an entire epoch, which includes
a series of pitiless class wars, not to mention civil wars, it
is indeed clear that the state can not die out in such a
situation. But as soon as the decisive world victory of the
proletariat appears, the growth curve of proletarian state-
hood begins to fall abruptly. For the essential and first task
of state power as such, the task of the suppression of the
bourgeoisie, will be over. External coercive measures will
begin to die out: first the armies and fleet will die out as
L 179 tools of the greatest external necessity; then the system of
punitive and repressive organs; further, the compulsory
character of labor, etc. Productive powers, which are distributed not according to state divisions but according to
the principle of economic expediency, are developed with
surprising rapidity. The colossal stores of energy which
were previously wasted on class struggle, war, militarism,
the overcoming of crises, competition, etc. are transformed
into productive labor. The deformation of classes and the
education of labor as well as the education of new gen-
erations and the rationalizing of the whole process of production accelerate even further the growth of productive
powers. Distribution loses the character of compulsory
equivalence-distribution "according to ability." Socialism
of the proletarian dictatorship and the other periods are
developed into a system of communist society.[147] For the

172

first time since humanity existed, a system arises which is constructed harmonically in all its parts: it knows neither social hierarchy nor hierarchy of production. It annihilates once and for all the struggle of people against people and welds the entire human race into a community which rapidly seizes the countless riches of nature.

The proletariat, which actively builds the future of humanity and clearly sees this future, can say with the words of the great pioneers of science: *Novarum rerum mihi nascitur ordo*. Even if the blind do not see this new order—its coming is inevitable and not to be deflected.

FOOTNOTES

[1] Marx, *Capital*, Vol. I, English edition, Moscow, 1966, p. 75.

[2] In a much worse but more eccentric manner, Heinrich Diezel develops the same thoughts about this, in *Theoretische Sozialökonomik*. Cf. also P. Struve, *Economy and Price* (Russian).

[3] Dr. Karl von Tyszka, *Das weltwirtschaftliche Problem der modernen Industrie-Staaten*, Jena, 1916, p. 1.

[4] Bernhard Harms, *Volkswirtschaft und Weltwirtschaft*, Jena, Gustav Fischer, 1912.

[5] Kobatsch, *La politique économique internationale* Paris, Girard et Brière.

[6] Carl Diehl, "Privatwirtschaftslehre, Volkswirtschaftslehre, Weltwirtschaftslehre," in *Conrads Jahrbücher*. B. Harms, "Volkswirtschaft und Weltwirtschaft" (Antikritische Darlegungen), in *Weltwirtschaftliches Archiv*, 1914, 1, p. 196 ff.

[7] This concept has been introduced by the author of this book. See N. Bukharin, *World Economy and Imperialism*, Petersburg, 1918.

[8] The question of division of labor has been researched to a relatively small extent, but in relation to the different character of labor, there is complete agreement. Cf. William Petty, *The Economic Writing*, Vol. I: *Political Arithmetic*, p. 260 ff.; same author, *Another Essay in Political Arithmetic* (Vol. II of his *Works*, p. 473 ff.); Adam Smith, *An Inquiry into the Nature*, Book I, Chapter I ("The Separation of Different Trades and Employments from One Another"). Marx, *Capital*, Vol. I; also more recent authors. Cf. Gustav Schmoller, "Die Tatsachen der Arbeitsteilung," *Jahrbücher*, 1889; same author, "Das Wesen der Arbeitsteilung und der sozialen Klassenbildung," *Jahrbücher*, 1890; Emile Durkheim, *De la division du travail social*, Paris, 1893 (an outstanding work devoted specifically to this question); J. B. Clark, *The Distribution of Wealth*, New York, 1908, p. 11-12; J. Fisher, *Elementary Principles of Economics*, New York, 1912, p. 193; F. Oppenheimer *(Theorie der reinen und politischen Oekonomic)* believes himself original when he introduces a division of labor . . . between the worker and the machine! (p. 115 ff) Lexis' classifications are interesting in *Allgemeine Volkswirtschaftslehre*.

[9] Marx, *Capital*, Vol. III, English, Moscow, 1966, p. 173.

[10] Cf. our work: *World Economy and Imperialism*.

174

FOOTNOTES

11 Thomas Hobbes, *The Moral and Political Works*, London, 1750. "Non est potastas super terram quae comparetur ei." (Job. 4124)

12 *Marx* attributes great economic importance to war. Cf. his *Introduction to a Critique of Political Economy*. Sombart renders a completely distorted picture in his book, *Krieg und Kapitalismus*. One can find a critique of him in Kautsky, "*Krieg und Kapitalismus*," in the *Neue Zeit*, 1913, Vol. II, p. 39.

13 *Frederick Engels: The Origin of the Family, Private Property and the State*, Marx-Engels Selected Works (English edition), Moscow, 1968, p. 588. "Politics is nothing more than a method of persistence, an instrument of maintaining the extension of property." *(Achille Loria: Les bases économiques de la constitution sociale*, 2nd ed., Paris, 1903, p. 362) | L 180

14 See Gumplowicz, *Geschichte der Staatstheorien*, Innsbruck, 1905, p. 8. Cf. also Loening, "Der Staat" in *Handwörterbuch der Staatswissenschaft*; Wygodzinsky, "Staat und Wirtschaft" in *Handbuch der Politik*; Jerusalem, *Der Krieg im Zeichen der Gesellschaftslehre*, I., p. 61.

15 To one who became acquainted with the literature on population in connection with cries of the "degeneration of the nation," it is clear that a whole series of steps intended to prevent the "degeneration" is dictated by the desire to have the appropriate amount of usable cannon fodder.

16 Cf. Hans *Delbrück, Regierung und Volkswille*, p. 133: "Where does the true power finally rest? It rests in the arms. Thus the decisive question for the internal character of a state is always: To whom belongs the army?" Cf. this to the naive prophecies of Spencer's *Man Versus the State*. | L 181

17 The Social Democrats have completely distorted this point of view. The author of this work has already vigorously represented it at the beginning of the war in a series of newspaper and journal articles: in the Dutch *De Tribune* (article: "De Nieuwe Lyveigensckap," Nov. 25, 1916, etc.), in the organ of the Norwegian left, *Klassenkampen*, in the Bremen *Arbeiterpolitik*, and finally in the journal *Jugendinternationale* (Switzerland) as well as in polemical articles in the New York newspaper *Novi Mir*. From the works of the classics of Marxism, cf. Engels, *Origin . . .*; Engels, *Anti-Dühring*; Engels, "Dell, Autorità" (*Neue Zeit*, 32. I); Marx, *Critique of the Gotha Programme*; Marx, *Contribution to the Critique of Hegel's Philosophy of Right*, etc. An excellent elucidation of this question with a selection of corresponding quotations from Marx and Engels can be found in the work of Lenin, *State and Revolution*. No better than the Social Democrats did the bourgeois professors comprehend Marx's communist teaching. Thus, for example, Adolf Wagner ("Staat in nationalökonomischer Hinsicht" in the *Wörterbuch der Staatswissenschaften*) writes that the socialist "state" can have all characteristics of the state "in its highest potentiality," because the class character of the modern state is merely a product of "misuse" (just as in Böhm-

175

Bawerk, for whom usury is a "misuse" and for whom profit remains, even in the socialist state where profit will grow on trees). Jellinek (*Allgemeine Staatslehre*) "understands" Marx just as Wagner does. But the "theory of power" fills him with horror, and he declares that "its practical results" exist "not in the stabilization but in the destruction of the state" (p. 175) and that this theory would pave the way for the revolution in permanence. Cf. Gumplowicz, *Geschichte der Staatstheorien*, p. 373 ff.

L 182

[18] F. Oppenheimer, "Staat und Gesellschaft" in *Handbuch der Politik*, Vol. I, p. 117. Cf. also Oppenheimer, *Der Staat;* the same author, *Theorie der reinen und politischen Oekonomie*, 3rd ed., 1911.

[19] On this, cf. Engels, *Anti-Dühring;* Schmoller, *Das Wesen der Arbeitsteilung und Klassenbildung* (polemic against Gumplowicz on p. 72). Against this theory, the development in the United States is particularly emphasized, although North American feudalism must not be underestimated. See Gustavus Mayers, *The History of Great American Fortunes*.

[20] Werner Sombart in his already mentioned work, *Krieg und Kapitalismus*, gives a description of the influence of wars on the rise of capitalism itself. The method of Sombart, who lets different mothers (first war, then luxury, then love—cf. his book, *Luxus und Kapitalismus*), one after another, give birth to capitalism, according to the honorable Herr Professor's mood, inevitably entails, however, terrible exaggerations.

[21] Dr. Herbert von Beckerath, "Zwangskartellierung oder freie Organisation der Industrie," in *Finanz und Volkswirtschaftliche Zeitfragen*, ed. by Schanz and J. Wolf, No. 49, Stuttgart, 1918, p. 22. This bourgeois university lecturer naturally depicts, as is fitting for a head doorman of capitalism, the class state under the pseudonym of "peoples." On the other hand, he overlooks the fact that not only the "export markets" play a role, but also the raw material markets and the spheres of investment of capital, i.e. those very instances which correspond to the three parts of the formula:

$$M - C \left\{ \begin{array}{l} \text{Means of Production} \\ \text{Labour-power} \end{array} \right. \ \ldots P \ldots C' - M'$$

[21a] This is emphasized especially sharply by Arthur Feiler, editor of the *Frankfurter Zeitung*, in his work: *Vor der Uebergangswirtschaft*, Frankfurt, 1918, p. 33 ff. His formula is: "We have organized the deficiency." The question is taken much further by Emil Lederer (*Der Wirtschaftsprozess im Kriege*): "War used to be economically a problem of state finances. But today the state is omnipotent; therefore its operation does not appear outwardly in the form of an enterprise. It is no longer a finance-economic problem, no longer a monetary problem, but the natural substance of the entire political economy is mobilized for war." (p. 362)

[22] Cf. R. Hilferding, *Das Finanzkapital*, Chap. 9: "The Commodity Exchange." "But war economy closes the exchange, and therewith the

entire problematic was ended." (E. Lederer: *Der Wirtschaftsprozess im Kriege*).

²³ In her article, "The Deorganizational and Organizational Processes in the period of the Transformation Economy" (in the journal *Narodnoye Khozyaistvo*, No. 6. 1919), Comrade M. Smit distinguishes between "exchange which is based on the capital-creating function of money" (M — C — M') and exchange "for the purpose of trading one commodity for another," whereby state-capitalist distribution is supposed to constitute the transition from the first to the second. This is an incredible mishmash. First, money has never had a capital-creating "function" anywhere and does not have it now. Second, a transition to simple commodity economy (formula: M — C — M') in state-capitalist society is not existent at all. There is a tendency towards an elimination of the commodity economy within the country and to a change of form of surplus value. But this is a question of a totally different kind.

²⁴ On state capitalism, cf. besides the quoted works the following: F. Pinner. *Die Konjunktur des wirtschaftlichen Sozialismus, Die Bank* April, 1915; Prof. Jaffe. "Die Militarisierung unseres Wirtschaftslebens" in the *Archiv für Sozialwissenschaft und Sozialpolitik*, 1915. 40, Vol. 3, No. V; Guyot. "Les problèmes économiques après la guerre," *Journal des économistes*, Aug. 15, 1915; Prof. Karl Ballod. "Einiges aus der Utopienliteratur der letzen Jahre" in Grünberg's *Archiv für die Geschichte des Sozialismus*, Vol. 6. No. 1; Walter Rathenau, *Die neue Wirtschaft* and *Der neue Staat;* G. Bernhard. *Uebergangswirtschaft.* Berlin, 1918; "Monopolfrage und Arbeiterklasse" (collection of articles by right Social Democrats); from Russian works we refer to the articles and brochures of Comrade Larin (M. Lurje), especially on the organization of German industry. Cf. also N. Ossinski, *The Building of Socialism* (the first chapters).

²⁵ Of course such is the case with the "pure model" of state capitalism, which reveals itself in reality merely as a tendency.

²⁶ On Germany, cf. the data of Johann Müller in "Nationalökonomische Gesetzgebung." *Jahrbücher für Nationalökonomie und Staat*, 1915. On France, see Ch. Gide, "The Provisioning of France and Measures to that End" *(The Economic Journal*. March. 1916) and the data in the English journal, *The Economist (ibidem* on England).

²⁷ On legal norms and forms of state-capitalist relationships, cf. Prof. Hatschek, "Die Rechtstechnik des Kriegssozialismus" (*Deutsche Revue,* June, 1916).

²⁸ The terminology is here used in the sense of its use by Comrade A. Bogdanow. Cf. his article on the tendencies of proletarian culture in *Proletarian Culture*, also *General Theory of Organization* (Russian). | L 183

²⁹ Comrade A. Bogdanow would like to merely see "ration cards" in

the entire process of organization, i.e. merely the rationing process which has arisen from the decline of productive powers. But in reality the rationing process goes significantly deeper in importance. The decline of productive powers in no way precludes the progress of the organizational forms of capitalism. That was also the case in "normal times" but especially during the crises when the temporary decline of production powers was accompanied by an accelerated centralization of production and a rise of new capitalist organizations. The same error—mutatis mutandis—was committed by Engels, too, when he spoke of syndicates and trusts. This error must not be repeated now.

L 184

³⁰ One cannot, as Maslow (*The Agrarian Question,* Vol. 1: *Theory of the Unfolding of the Political Economy* and other works) does in his definition of productive powers, put the means of production and living labor in common parentheses, i.e. add a static quantity to a process. It is not labor which is adequate to the means of production but labor power. On production powers, cf. Marx, *Capital, The Poverty of Philosophy,* etc. Cf. also: "Production" in *Nouveau Dictionnaire d'écon. polit.* by Léon Say ("puissance productive . . . l'ensemile de ces éléments envisagés comme des forces"); Kleinwächter, "Die volkswirtschaftliche Produktion im allgemeinen" in Schönberg's *Handbuch;* B. Harms, "Arbeit" in the *Handwörterbuch der Staatswissenschaften;* Lexis, "Produktion," *ibidem;* Lexis, *General Theory of Political Economy,* 1910; Watkins' "Third Factor in Variation of Productivity," in *The American Economic Review,* December, 1915 (Vol. V, No. 4); F. Oppenheimer, *Theorie der reinen und politischen Oekonomie,* the section on "Die produktiven Kräfte" (p. 138-139 ff.); R. Hilferding, *Eine neue Untersuchung über die Arbeitsmittel.* Exact formulations are found in Rodbertus, *Zur Beleuchtung der sozialen Frage,* Part 1, 1890, p. 60. ("Productive power and productivity must be distinguished. Productivity means the effectiveness or fruitfulness of the productive power." In other words, Rodbertus takes the productive powers *in natura*). Cf. also Liszt, *Das nationale System der politischen Oekonomie.*

³¹ Rosa Luxemburg, *The Accumulation of Capital,* p. 1.

³² See Marx, *Capital,* Vols. II and III.

³³ Mr. P. Struve has intentionally banned production relations from his analysis in his work, *Economy and Value* (Russian), in order to be able to assert that social class relations are an eternal attribute of every society. On this, cf. our article, "The Feats of Mr. Struve," in the Marxist journal *Proswestshenye,* No. 129, 1913.

³⁴ Cf. Marx, *The Poverty of Philosophy.*

³⁵ Unfortunately, even many comrades do not comprehend this and attribute to relative laws of specific historical significance a supernatural, absolute reality. Even the embryonic social bookkeeping of the socialist

178

FOOTNOTES

economy "is based" with us on this erroneous conception. And this happens at the very period where the value-expression of money is incommensurate with the real labor process and where the latter does not regulate the distribution of productive powers.

36 R. Goldscheid, *Staatssozialismus oder Staatskapitalismus*. A finance-sociological contribution to the solution of the problem of state debts. 4th and 5th eds., Vienna-Leipzig, 1917.

37 On this, cf. the work by Comrade N. Lenin, *State and Revolution*, as well as our article: "Theory of the Proletarian Dictatorship" in the omnibus edition, *The October Revolution and the Dictatorship of the Proletariat* (Russian).

38 R. Hilferding, *Finanzkapital, Marxstudien*, Vienna, 1910, pp. 472-3.

39 Prof. Grinewetzki, *The Post-War Perspectives of Russian Industry* (Russian).

40 As befits an apologist of capitalism, Prof. Grinewetzki in his book considers the question exclusively from the point of view of capitalist production relations, as an eternal, universal category of human existence. To the future historicist of ideologies, that true blindness of a chicken, which distinguished the bourgeois scholars in an age of the greatest social upheavals, will appear transparently funny. L 185

41 The theoreticians of castrated Marxism, like Kautsky, have a truly childish conception of revolutionary upheavals. For them, theoretical and practical problems which pose the greatest difficulty simply do not exist; they pass disdainfully over empirically given facts by registering the really occurring revolutions under "unreal" and "incorrect"—a method which from the Marxist point of view itself deserves the most severe contempt. E.g., cf. Karl Kautsky, *The Dictatorship of the Proletariat; Terrorism and Communism; The Socialization of Agriculture*, "Preface." A temporary decline of productive powers which, objectively considered, in the last analysis extended their strength, occurred also in the bourgeois revolutions. (Great French Revolution, Civil War in America, etc.) See N. Bukharin, "The Dictatorship of the Russian Proletariat and the World Revolution," *Communist International*, Nos. 4 and 5.

42 Comrade Kritzmann has referred to this side of the question in a different formulation of the question, indeed. ("Basic Tendencies of the Social Revolution of the Proletariat" in *Narodnoye Khosyaistvo*, No. 3, 1919). With him, as with most authors, the capitalist organization of social economy falls away like a *shell* . . . "it is on the whole a simple replacement of the leading powers" . . . (p. 14). The partial disintegration of the proletariat as a class, which takes place under the influence of the decline of productive powers as a result of a repelling of the proletariat and a reduction of production, is a phenomenon of another kind.

43 Therefore the liberal professors and their opportunistic parrots, who

179

do not want to see socialism but want to justify this fact for mere form's sake with allegedly "scientific" arguments, interpret Marx in their own way. E.g., thus Franz Oppenheimer teacher of P. Maslow, writes: "The tremendous superiority in numbers and force of the proletariat . . . expropriates the expropriators, who are able to offer no serious resistance, and takes over the completely finished mechanism of production and distribution, which continues to run unchanged and unshaken . . . That is the Marxian theory of socialization." Franz Oppenheimer, "Zur Theorie und Vergesellschaftung," in the omnibus edition, *Wege und Ziele der Sozialisierung*, ed. by Dr. Hermann Beck. (Cf. *Bund Neues Vaterland*, Berlin, p. 16.) Dr. Prange (see the same book) calls this a "clear representation of Marxist theory" (p. 79). The honorable professors obviously believe that the stock exchange, stock-jobbing, and speculation are just as characteristic for socialist society as virtue is for the Holy Virgin, and that the birth of the socialist apparatus of production and distribution disturbs the capitalist virginity not in the least. They are echoed by Otto Bauer: "It (expropriation) can not and should not be executed in the form of a brutal (!) confiscation . . . for in this form it could not be executed other than at the price of a violent devastation of the means of production, which would impoverish the masses of people and bury the sources of national income. The expropriation of the expropriators should rather be executed in an ordered, regulated way; in such a way that the apparatus of production of the society is not destroyed, and the business of industry and of agriculture is not hindered." (Otto Bauer, *Der Weg zum Sozialismus*, Berlin, 1919, p. 28.) The former "minister of socialization" obviously does not want to build socialism from earthly but rather from heavenly elements.

[44] "The monopoly of capital becomes a fetter upon the mode of production, which has sprung up and flourished along with, and under it. *Centralization of the means of production and socialization of labor* at last reach a point where they become incompatible with their capitalist integument. Thus integument is burst asunder. The knell of capitalist private property sounds. The expropriators are expropriated." Karl Marx, *Capital*, (English edition), Vol. I, p. 763.

[45] "Personen- und Sachapparat" (Dr. Hermann Beck, *Sozialisierung als organisatorische Aufgabe*, p. 32 of the quoted omnibus volume).

[46] In *The Poverty of Philosophy* Marx speaks of the "organization of the revolutionary elements as a class." In the *Communist Manifesto* we find the following description of the cooperative relations of the workers: "Wage labour is based *exclusively* (emphasis ours, N.B.) on competition between the labourers. The advance of industry . . . replaces the isolation of the labourers, due to competition, by their revolutionary combination, due to association. The development of Modern Industry, therefore, cuts from under its feet, the very foundation on which the bourgeoisie produces and appropriates products. What the bourgeoisie, therefore, pro-

duces, above all, are its own grave-diggers." Marx quotes this passage in the footnote at the end of Chapter 32 of the first volume of *Capital*, (Foreign Languages Publishing House, p. 764). It is completely clear that Marx evaluates the proletariat not only as a power which brings about the "violent overthrow," but also as the social embodiment of co-operative relations which grow within capitalism and create the base for the socialist (alias communist) mode of production. E. Hammacher (*Das Philosophisch-ökonomische System des Marxismus*, Leipzig. 1909) would have us believe that Marx developed this point of view in *The Poverty of Philosophy* and in the *Communist Manifesto* in contradiction to *Capital*. That is evidently the reason that Marx quotes the corresponding passages in *Capital!*

47 *Capital*, Vol. I, p. 763.

48 The immeasurable public meanness of the opportunistic theories exists in the very fact that they come to terms with state capitalism and protest against socialism, which they are several times ready to accept *in words*, outside of praxis. | L 186

49 Above all by *Kautsky*. Before the war he "waited" for the catastrophe, which was not yet "mature." During the war he warned against the revolution, for he said that the International was an "instrument of peace" and would fail upon the thunder of cannons. After the war he warned against socialism, for the catastrophe would have an "exhausting" effect. One can only say, what a unified conception! | L 187

50 On this, cf. N. Ossinski, *The Building of Socialism* (Russian), Chap. I; also Bukharin, *World Economy and Imperialism*, Petrograd, 1918. The following prediction by Engels is interesting: "The colossal expansion of the means of transportation and communication—ocean liners, railways, electrical telegraph, the Suez Canal—has made a real world-market a fact. The former monopoly of England in industry has been challenged by a number of competing industrial countries; infinitely greater and varied fields have been opened in all parts of the world for the investment of surplus European capital, so that it is far more widely distributed and local over-speculation may be more easily overcome. By means of all this, most of the old breeding-grounds of crises and opportunities for their development have been eliminated or strongly reduced. At the same time, competition in the domestic market recedes before the cartels and trusts, while in the foreign market it is restricted by protective tariffs. . . . But these protective tariffs are nothing but preparations for the ultimate general industrial war, which shall decide who has supremacy on the world-market. Thus every factor, which works against a repetition of the old crises, carries within itself the germ of a far more powerful future crisis." (*Capital*, Vol. III, English edition, p. 489, footnote.) | L 188

51 The fairly numerous "investigations" into "socialization," originated by bourgeois professors, naturally evade this basic question. See K. | L 189

Bücher, *Die Sozialisierung;* Tübingen, 1919; Otto Neurath, *Wesen und Weg der Sozialisierung;* Prof. K. Tyszka, *Die Sozialisierung des Wirtschaftslebens,* Jena, 1919. Also cf. Otto Bauer, *loc. cit.;* Rudolf Goldscheid, *Sozialisierung der Wirtschaft oder Staatsbankerott.* From communist literature of foreign countries, we can name the brochures of a Hungarian comrade and engineer—Julius Hevesi, *Die Technische und Wirtschaftliche Notwendigkeit der Kommunistischen Weltrevolution,* Vienna, 1919.

[52] Rudolf Goldscheid censures most ingeniously the cowardly attitude of the "leaders": "It is simply unbelievable with which obviously untenable arguments one is now capable of successfully delaying the acceleration of the socialization of the economy. Thus, for example, by asserting that, because momentarily all of production and business is at a standstill and the necessary means of business are lacking, that this would be the most inappropriate moment to socialize the economy. If, on the other hand, the economy were in the greatest boom, one would doubtlessly declare that one dare not try any experiments while everything is going so smoothly. One always finds good reasons against something one doesn't want. And in any case it is obvious that in a period where business has slackened and where a far-reaching reconversion of the economy appears unavoidable under all circumstances, it would be desirable to effect the transformation of the individualistic into the socialist economy as soon as possible." (*Sozialisierung der Wirtschaft oder Staatsbankerott,* Vienna, 1919, p. 11) This is written—ad notam of the Social Democracy— by a bourgeois pacifist.

[53] The scholars of the bourgeoisie were stupefied by fetishistic poison to such a degree that they exalted capitalist confusion as a pearl of creation. Thus Mr. P. Struve denied in principle the possibility of rationalizing the economic process and confessed to a "scientific conviction of the basic and immanent dualism of this process." (*Economy and Value,* Vol. I, Russian, p. 60.) Truly, the wish is father to the thought!

[54] N. Ossinski, "On the Presuppositions of Socialist Revolution," in *Narodnoye Khosyaistvo* (Russian), No. 6-7, p. 5, 1918. Marx foresaw correctly the wearisome character of the catastrophe and the transformation period. In the *Disclosures about the Trial of Communists in Cologne,* he quotes his words: "We . . . tell the workers: you will have to go through 15, 20, 50 years of civil wars and national struggles, not only to change conditions but also to change yourselves."

[55] Hermann Beck, "Eröffnungsansprache" (*Wege und Ziele der Sozialisierung,* pp. 10-12). Incidentally, the way in which Herr Beck treats the revolution is very reminiscent of our holy "Novaya Zhisn."

[56] This formulation was given for the first time by Comrade Kritzman in an ingenious article, "On the Task at Hand of the Proletarian Revolu-

182

tion in Russia." (*Narodnoye Khosyaistvo*, 1918, No. 5).

[57] A sample of such theoretical improprieties is found unfortunately in the last (1918) "Works" of Professor R. J. Wipper. In the omnibus volume, *Untergang der Europäischen Kultur*, which appeared under the publishers "Knowledge is Power" (there is to find neither power nor knowledge), the honorable professor, without understanding the *perspectives*, gives a generalization of the first phases of the process and thereby expresses things which seem downright funny. "The belief in the union of proletarians of all countries has disappeared . . . The expectation of an early social revolution is past . . . The capitalist class . . . is preparing for no inevitable decline . . ." (p. 75 of the omnibus volume) This appeared in 1918! In the article, "Sozializmus oder Kleinbürgertum," in which the brave author criticizes the Commune and calumniates it with a zeal worthy of a finer matter, and in which, in the name of the Paris Communards, the Russian Communists are actually depicted, we find, for example, this question: "Why did they (the Communards, read: the Bolsheviks) not attempt to agitate for intensified work, especially now that many factory owners have left the city and consequently the 'exploiters,' who 'suppressed' the workers, have disappeared; why did they support idleness and shiftlessness?" etc. etc. Doesn't this already sound funny in 1920, the year of the labor army, of Communist Saturdays, of labor discipline? "The spice of the country," as the Professor modestly labels himself, possesses a downright chicken "intellect," at least in a specific, historical epoch.

[58] On the characterization of these, cf. the author's book: N. Bukharin, *The Political Economy of the Leisure Class*.

[59] We say "state-economic," for at this stage of development "economics" merges with "politics" and the state loses its exclusively political character by also becoming an organ of economic administration.

[60] "Capitalism has created a large class of industrial and commercial leaders" (Marx) who constitute a particular category of specialists in the service of the bourgeoisie. This industrial bureaucracy does not belong directly to the class of capitalists but is bound to it with the tightest of bonds. It is educated by the bourgeoisie, draws its executive salary from it, has a share in the profits of flotation and in the distribution of dividends, invests its "savings" in stocks and shares, and to the degree that capital is depersonalized in stock companies, to the degree that clever business people, who know how to take advantage of *others'* capital, gain increasingly greater influence, this bureaucracy becomes more and more tightly joined to the capitalist "family" and is permeated by its interests.

And therefore it is necessary, if its services are to be used—and this is inevitable and necessary—that the soil, the milieu, with which it has intergrown, be eliminated as well. "One must not leave it in its former social connection." (N. Ossinski, *loc. cit.*, p. 54-55.) Cf. also the article of

Comrade M. Windelbot, "The Trusts and Syndicates and the Modern Production Associations" (Russian) in *Narodnoye Khosyaistvo*, 1919, No. 6, especially p. 31.

[61] From this point of view, the principal difference is also clear which exists between the retention of the old specialists by the Noske-Scheidemann Government and their employment in the building of the Soviet Republic. There they are in their former "social connection" and under the conditions of the democratized bourgeois power; here they are engaged in another connection and under the rule of the proletariat. There they are left in the "positions." Here they *return* merely *formally* to the "old" positions and to an important degree with a new consciousness. Comrade Ossinski notes with total correctness, "It is inadmissible that they (i.e. the specialists) be representatives of a hostile class, mediators between the proletarian dictatorship and finance capital." (*loc. cit.*, p. 56) In their dialectical *"return"* this is in praxis excluded, for this presupposes the disintegration of the old social production connections as well as the disintegration of the old personality of the technological mental laborers. The reader will of course comprehend that we are not speaking of sharply demarcated periods but of fluent processes, of "tendencies."

[62] *Capital*, Vol. I, English edition, Moscow, p. 180.

[63] In his *System der Organisationslehre*, Engineer Beck distinguishes two groups within the "technological means": the "means of information" and the "means of activity," especially the means of labor. To the "means of information" belong, among other: "Design, color, picture, writing, and language." (*Sozialisierung als Organisatorische Aufgabe*, p. 38). The experience of the Russian Revolution confirms perfectly the deductively derived statements of the text. One of the oldest syndicates, the sugar syndicate, collapsed into an organization of individual factories. The same is also the case with others. On metallurgy, cf. Windelbot, *loc. cit.*, *Narodnoye Khosyaistvo*, 1919, Nos. 6 and 9-10.

[64] In the second edition of his book, *Syndicates and Trusts in Russia* (Russian), Moscow, 1919, Comrade G. *Zyperovitsh* demonstrates vividly how greatly the customary conceptions of "organic" epochs weigh even on people who think in revolutionary terms. His theoretical constructions do not represent the economic organizations of the proletarian administration as *new* apparatus but as apparatus which derive their origin from the apparatus of the bourgeoisie. Nevertheless, *every sentence* of the factual material which he himself introduces stands in striking contradiction to this conception and confirms absolutely *our* point of view. This is also logically related to the terrible, theoretical muddle in the general estimation of the epoch, of which we will occasionally still speak in another chapter. We want to bring examples. Comrade Zyperovitsh writes the following on the Supreme Council for economy and on councils for

economy in general: "These supreme organs of economic administration of the country, which have been formed from representatives of workers organizations and which have solely trustees of the party centers at their head, were actually the successors of the economic council of the provisory government." (I.e. the government of Kerenski and Co.) What does that mean? And what is to be understood by "successorship"? It is clear that we are here dealing with a total *destruction* of the old and the creation of a completely *new* organization. The "actual" exists solely in the administrative function. Comrade Zyperovitsh, however, speaks of syndicates as well as trusts in the Soviet Republic as old apparatus, in which merely "the content itself . . . must become essentially different." (p. 170) Comrade Zyperovitsh does not notice at all that our production associations are completely *different* organizational apparatus, that they have grown up *on the skeleton* of the dead, decayed, disintegrated capitalist apparatus. We urge our readers to study from this point of view the last chapters of Zyperovitsh's book in order to convince themselves once again of the complete naiveté of the old concepts.

[65] The Social Democratic opportunists directly defame the revolutionary Marxist method when they maintain that a change of functions means an alteration in the *class* characteristics. The proletariat wages a class struggle in the epoch of dictatorship, but it wages it as the ruling class, as the organizing and creating, the building class, of the new society. Nonetheless, this ABC of Marxism is a profound mystery to all apologists of "healthy capitalism."

[66] The slow-witted "critics" from the right like to ridicule our unions, newspapers, and festivities as "official," but they shamefully suppress the fact that in the dictatorship of the proletariat, the officiality is *proletarian*. Thereby the fervent wish is cloaked that the "office" constantly find itself in the hands of the class enemy of the proletariat.

[67] Marx, *Capital*, Vol. I, p. 352.

[68] It by no means follows from this, as Kautsky believes (see his articles on Imperialism in the *Neue Zeit*), that the roots of imperialism lie exclusively in this sphere. From the point of view of conditions of reproduction, the change in all three parts of the formula is important:

$$M - C \left\{ \begin{matrix} \text{Labour-power} \\ \text{Means of Production} \end{matrix} \right. \quad \ldots \ P \ldots \ C' - M'$$

$$\underbrace{\qquad\qquad}_{\text{I}} \quad \underbrace{\quad}_{\text{II}} \ \underbrace{\quad}_{\text{III}}$$

To the first part of the formula correspond the "raw materials markets" and the markets of "cheap labor power," to the second the spheres of investment of capital, and finally to the third the outlet markets. The change takes place in these *three* areas and the struggle between imperialist bodies correspondingly is executed along three lines.

[69] Emil Lederer ("Die ökonomische Umschichtung im Krieg," *Archiv für Sozialwissenschaft und Politik, Krieg und Wirtschaft*, No. 7, 1918,

p. 34) cites the following table, which illustrates the "displacement of profitability":

	Gross Income	Expenses	Net Profit
Before the war	100	75	25
Present minimum	200	96	105
Probable average	250	95	155
Maximum	300	95	205

"Through the far higher prices attained in the black market . . . still higher returns were effected." Since the difference grows larger between the prices in "free" trade and the highest prices, the real "displacement" is of course much greater.

70 On this, cf. the brochure of Comrade J. Larin: "The Utopians of Minimalism and the Reality," Petrograd, 1917 (Russian). In this brochure Comrade Larin notes with complete correctness: "In short, if agriculture itself was not sufficiently ripened *from within* with respect to organization, then modern German capitalism produced a sufficient store of material and social organizational powers to fuse agriculture from the top down and from without, and to unite it into a unified, systematically administrated organism. In other words, one must not consider the material 'ripeness' of the country from the point of view of the necessity to first bring every branch of the economy in itself to technological-organizational ripeness but rather as a derivative of the general condition of all its productive powers in their average." (p. 17-18)

71 Karl Kautsky writes in his booklet, *Die Sozialisierung der Landwirtschaft* (Berlin, 1919): "The revolution in the cities has not passed by the workers on the open land without a trace. There would be unspeakable mischief afoot if they were also to be seized with strike fever (!) . . ." (p. 10) Kautsky is right when he goes on to warn against the division of the large estates among the farm workers. But to protest against "strike fever" means to crouch before the Prussian *Junker*. The fall of capitalism in the country is as important a link in the chain of the general process as in the city. In the advanced capitalist states, a victory of the working class without training the masses of the country proletariat ("strike fever," as Kautsky says; "strike hazard" was once said by our Mensheviks) is unthinkable, for the agrarian—even if it be Mr. von Tūnen—will never voluntarily want to realize Kautsky's program. The misunderstanding of this situation, the elimination of class struggle, is the basic sin of Kautsky and accomplices. Also cf. Otto Bauer, *Der Weg zum Sozialismus.*

72 Here one can draw an analogy between the depicted process and the disintegration of relationships between advanced mother countries and their colonies. The colonial uprisings contain in themselves, objectively speaking the possibility of a new capitalist cycle of development,

when one observes this process in an isolated way. But in the general complex of phenomena, this is a by-product as well as simultaneously the strongest factor of the disintegration of the imperialist system, as a precondition of the socialist rebirth of humanity.

73 Cf. the article of Comrade Hoichbarg, "The Socialization of Agriculture" in *Nar. Khos.*, 1919, No. 5; also Miljutin, "Socialism and Agriculture"; N. Bogdanow, "Organization of the Soviet Economies" in *Nar. Khos.*, 1919, No. 6.

74 Kautsky is therefore correct when he writes in (*Sozialisierung der Landwirtschaft*, Foreword, p. 12): "For us the agrarian question is the most complicated, but also the most important, of the revolution." However, the entire misfortune of Kautsky exists in the fact that he neither sees nor understands the entire *complicatedness* of the problem. For him there is not the basic "complicating" factor: the class struggle of the various social groups. This is logically connected to the failure to understand the fact that production relations of capitalist society are simultaneously class relations and technological labor relations as well. | L 190

75 The "sociologist" *Kautsky* doesn't comprehend this at all. In the foreword to his work, *Sozialisierung der Landwirtschaft*, already quoted by us, he attacks the Bolsheviks because they did not let the peasantry be their own master (p. 10), and he here reveals his complete ignorance (for he isn't even familiar with Soviet farm conditions). But one page further (p. 11) he rails at them because they "oppress" the peasantry and take from it the surplus for the needs of the cities and the army. The "clever" Kautsky does not even comprehend the meaning of the war against Denikin, does not understand what the most uneducated peasant understands. The naked fury against the party of revolutionary communism dictates thoughts to him which would be worthy of a high-school freshman from a "good family." | L 191

76 "In view of the prevailing small business, this (i.e. socialization. N.B.) will have to be considered, at least at first, more as a regulation of the circulation process between city and country than as an organizing of production." (Kautsky, *loc. cit.*, p. 9) | L 192

77 N. Lenin, "Economics and Politics in the Epoch of the Dictatorship of the Proletariat," *Communist International*, 1919, No. 6 (Russian edition, p. 890).

78 *ibidem*, p. 891.

79 *The Poverty of Philosophy*, English edition, Marxist Library, Vol. XXVI, New York, p. 112.

80 Cf., e.g., *Capital*, Vol. I, also Vol. III, part 1, where an analysis of the average rate of profit is given. Example: "With the productive power of labour increases the mass of products, in which a certain value, and, therefore, a surplus-value of a given magnitude, is embodied. The more

L 193 the productive power of labour rises, the more means of consuming and accumulating does the surplus-value encompass." Or clearer: "That part of constant capital, which A. Smith calls the fixed, the instruments of labour, the buildings, machinery and the like, functions always completely in the production process but depreciates only gradually and transfers only from time to time its value to the commodities which in the long run it helps to produce. It constitutes a true measure of the *progress of the productive forces.*" Quite the same in *Theories of Surplus Value,* under "Productive power or power of labour." Different: "Productive power" ("means of production") in the "Introduction to A Critique of Political Economy." [Note by the editor of this English edition: Bukharin here and in most other cases quotes *Capital* in German, but from Kautsky's Popular Edition which in many parts differs from Marx's wordings. Wherever possible, we are using the standard English edition, published in Moscow, but for these quotes only the very first sentence is to be found in the edition which was authorized by Engels, see I, p. 604.]

[81] G. Rodbertus-Jagetzow, *Zur Beleuchtung der sozialen Frage,* Berlin, 1890, pp. 60-61. Also cf. the literature on productive powers in Chapter III of this work.

[82] Marx, *Theories of Surplus Value,* English edition, Moscow, 1968, Part II, p. 510.

[83] The author vigorously emphasized this point of view in his book, *World Economy and Imperialism.* Cf. *The Communist Manifesto* (in: *Selected Works of Marx and Engels,* Moscow, 1968), p. 41: "And how does the bourgeoise get over these crises? On the one hand by enforced destruction of a mass of productive forces; on the other, by the conquest of new markets, and by the thorough exploitation of the old ones. That is to say, by paving the way for more extensive and more destructive crises, and by diminishing the means whereby crises are prevented."

[84] *Theories of Surplus Value,* Part II (Chap. XVII), English edition, Moscow, 1968, pp. 495-6.

L 194 [85] Well-known is the destruction caused by the Civil War in America— a war which has provided a powerful impulse to the development of capitalism. Well-known is the disorganization in the period of the French Revolution, which drove forward the development of productive powers after a period of their deep decline. Well-known is also the fact that the French Jacobins, who constituted the most active factor of the revolutionary movement, were accused of exactly the same sins as today's Communists. Following are excerpts from the trial of *Charlotte Corday,* the murderess of Marat:

"What motive could have prompted you to decide upon such a terrible act?

188

FOOTNOTES

"His crimes.

"Which crimes do you charge him with?

"The impoverishment of France and the Civil War which he kindled in the entire country.

"With what do you substantiate these accusations?

"His former crimes are the informants of his present crimes. It was he who instigated the September murders; he fanned the flames of the Civil War, in order to be established as dictator or something, and it was he again who infringed upon the sovereignty of the people by attaining the arrest and incarceration of the deputies of the Convent." ("The Revolutionary Tribunal at the Time of the Great French Revolution," *Recollections of Contemporaries and Documents,* Russian edition, ed. by Prof. Tarlé, Part I, p. 59.)

Is not this dialogue between a revolutionary Jacobin and a counter-revolutionary Girondist lady the prototype of a "dialogue" between a Communist and a Social Democrat? Not for nothing did *Plekhanov* predict in the *"Iskra"* for the 20th century a split of Socialists into "Montagnards" and "Girondists." This prophecy came into effect with astronomical exactitude, and the Messrs. Kautsky and accomplices show off in the entire costume of the virtuous and not too clever Girondists. Once Kautsky defended the Jacobins. But what can one do? "Nous avons changé tout cela."

[86] Comrade L. Kritzmann (Cf. his article, "The Development of Productive Powers and the Dictatorship of the Proletariat" in the omnibus volume: *Two Years of Dictatorship of the Proletariat,* Russian, p. 70) says with complete correctness: "But the proletariat differs from other productive powers (machines, materials, etc.) in that it responds with revolt to the threatening disorganization. The period of the crisis is a period of the growth of revolutionary revolt within the proletariat. *The revolution of the proletariat itself is nothing more than the reaction of the proletariat against the efforts of the bourgeoisie to minimize the* | L 195 *waste and the inactivity of the powers belonging to them by destroying the labor power of the proletariat, an effort to liquidate the crisis* which was engendered by the capitalist mode of production." (emphasis ours. N. B.)

[87] Cf. Marx, *The Poverty of Philosophy, loc. cit.,* p. 146: "Of all the instruments of production, the greatest productive power is the revolutionary class itself. The organization of revolutionary elements as a class supposes the existence of all the productive forces which could be engendered in the bossom of the old society." | L 196

[88] From this point of view it is absolutely meaningless to hold the working class and its party responsible for the destruction. For they are the very power which makes possible the reconstruction of society. On the resistance of the "old order"—on this alone—must the destruction during the transition period be blamed. | L 197

189

89 The Messrs. "Critics" of the proletarian revolution see in the destruction proof for the immaturity of the capitalist relationships. From our analysis we see that even under the "most mature" conditions a (transitory) disorganization is unavoidable. The "critics" often quote Marx's words (Marx, Contribution to the Critique, "Preface," in *Selected Works*, English edition, Moscow, 1968, p. 183): "No social order ever perishes before all the productive forces for which there is room in it have developed; and new, higher relations of production never appear before the material conditions of their existence have matured in the womb of the old society itself." However, Marx then immediately draws the conclusion: "Therefore mankind always sets itself only such tasks as it can solve; since, looking at the matter more closely, it will always be found that the task itself arises only when the material conditions for its solution already exist or are at least in the process of formation." The reduction of productive powers in the process of the proletarian revolution was theoretically foreseen by Comrade J. Larin in the already mentioned brochure, *The Utopians of Minimalism and the Reality* (Russian).

90 Prof. Grinevetski (*Postwar Perspectives of Russian Industry*, Moscow, 1919, p. 64, Russian) states this in the chapter, "The Revolutionary Disintegration of Industry," through the influence of the following factors: "1) the *complete disorganization of the supply of raw materials and fuel* as a result of the decrease in their yield and the obstruction of traffic; 2) the *labor crisis* as a result of the general disorganization under the influence of the revolution and the class war and the sinking of productivity as a result of different causes; 3) *technical disorganization*, in the material as well as in the administrative-technological aspect . . .; 4) the *extraordinary instability and stagnation of the market* . . .; 5) the *catastrophic course of demobilization* . . . as a result of the technical disorganization and the financial collapse of industry; 6) the *financial collapse of industry* as a result of the higher paying of labor and its lesser productivity, the absolute disorganization of supplies, the nationalizing of the banks, etc." One can easily be persuaded from this that all these factors are also included in our classification. But Mr. Grinevetski places the guilt not on the capitalist system with its war and its *thwarting* of the new society, but rather on the working class. Of course, an apologist of capitalism cannot act any differently, before whom "postwar perspectives" blossom as *capitalist perspectives*. Actually the same thing is said by Mr. Hoover, the "food dictator" of Europe (*National Food Journal*, Aug. 13, 1919): "The economic difficulties of Europe as a whole at the signature of peace may be almost summarized in the phrase: 'demoralized productivity.' It is not necessary to review at length the cause of this decrease of productivity. They are, in the main, as follows: 'The *industrial and commercial demoralization arising originally out of the war, but continued out of the struggle for political rearrangements* during the armistice, the creation of new Governments, their inexperience,

190

and frictions between these governments in the readjustment of economic relations. *The proper and insistent demand of labour for higher standards of living* and a voice in the administration in their effort has unfortunately (!!) become impregnated with the theory that the limitation of effort below physical necessity will increase the total employment or improve their condition. There is a great *relaxation of effort as the reflex of physical exhaustion* of large sections of the population from privation and from the mental and physical strain of the war. To a minor degree, considering the whole volume, there has been a destruction of equipment and tools, and the loss of organization . . ., due to war diversions, with a loss of man-power. . . . The *demoralization in the production of coal.* . . . It is due a small percentage—from the destruction of man-power to the physical limitation of coal mines or their equipment. It is due in the largest degree to the human factor of the limitation of the effort. The *continuation of the blockade* . . . has undoubtedly destroyed enterprise even in open countries' . . . etc." All these causes engender a "political, moral and economic chaos."

In a work on the postwar situation of world economy, writes O. C. Roedder, *Nacht und Morgen der Weltwirtschaft*, (Chemnitz): "Everything now depends on the German worker alone. It sounds like mockery to speak of the resumption of export when the worker within is unemployed" (p. 49). We hear analogous testimony from the American financier Vanderlip. Cf. also the report by A. Selenko, "Memorandum on the Question of Crediting of Russian Cooperation in North America." Of course all these gentlemen see merely the "laziness of the working class," without noticing the sabotage of the producers. They believe in their simplicity that the class struggle which is waged in the womb of the production process is a one-sided act, that it is waged merely by the workers, while the capitalists sit on the "universally human" throne and rigorously preserve the "interests of production" "in itself," the interests "of pure production." In reality, however, the pure reason of production bears all the traits of impure practical reason, which jingles its purse and looks very little like the Platonic "idea."

[91] An expression which was suggested by W. M. Smirnov (in the | L 198 weekly magazine of *Pravda*).

[92] Marx, *Capital*, Vol. I, p. 716.

[93] Marx already saw this in the *Communist Manifesto*.

[94] These tasks are technically necessary for every social model of economic rebirth. Cf., e.g., Grinevetski, *loc. cit.*; S. I. Gussev, "The Tasks at Hand of the Economic Building," *Materials of the Ninth Congress of the Russian Communist Party*. Cf. also the theses of the Central Committee of the Russian Communist Party at the Ninth Congress, as well as the newspaper, *Ekonomitsheskaya Shisn*.

[95] On this, cf. Marx, *Capital*; Kautsky, *Entwicklung und Vermehrung*,

191

etc.; J. Hevesi, "Die technische Notwendigkeit der kommunistischen Weltrevolution."

96 Cf. the brilliant brochure of Comrade Krshishanovski, engineer and electro-technician, on the electrification of Russian industry. Also W. A. Müller, "Sozialisierung des landwirtschaftlichen Verkehrswesens" in the omnibus edition, *Wege und Ziele der Sozialisierung*.

97 Bourgeois economists saw the cause of this in the "natural law" of the decreasing fertility of the soil, which was said to have a long "history" behind it. An excellent examination of this "law" is found in the work of Comrade N. Lenin, *The Agrarian Question and the Critics of Marx*. Bourgeois science, which represented this law as an imminent law of agricultural production, imputed to the social category the natural category—that is the basic "method" of this "science." A general characterization of the technical development is given by Marx from the angle of the relation between city and country in the *Theories of Surplus Value*, Part II, *loc. cit.*, pp. 109-110: "On the whole it can be assumed that under the cruder, pre-capitalist mode of production, agriculture is *more productive* than industry, because nature assists here as a machine and an organism, whereas in industry the powers of nature are still almost entirely replaced by human action (as in the craft type of industry etc.). In the period of the stormy growth of capitalist production, productivity in industry develops rapidly as compared with agriculture, although its development *presupposes* that a significant change as between constant and variable capital has already taken place in agriculture, that is, a large number of people have been driven off the land. Later, productivity advances in both, although at an uneven pace. But when industry reaches a certain level the disproportion must diminish, in other words, productivity in agriculture must increase relatively more rapidly than in industry."

98 *Grundlagen und Kritik des Sozialismus*, edited by Werner Sombart, Berlin, 1919, Part I, p. VII.

99 A French author defined imperialism as the effort of every form of life to extend itself at the cost of the others. From this point of view, the hen that doesn't even lay golden eggs but pecks at grain constitutes a subject of imperialistic policy, for it "annexes" this grain.

100 Cf. our article, "Some Basic Concepts of Modern Economics" in *Communist*, May 16, 1918, No. 3, p. 9 (Russian).

101 This thought, apparently so clear, remained unclear to many comrades. Thus, e.g., Comrade Cyperovitsh, in his already quoted work on the syndicates and trusts in Russia, wrote the following about the period after the October Revolution: "Even in the phase of preparation, which we are now going through, the phase of state capitalism (!!), the worker represents the master of production. . . ." (*loc. cit.*, p. 170). By what means the worker in the capitalist system can be the "master of pro-

duction"—that, of course, is not comprehensible to anyone, for such an extraordinary system is reminiscent of wooden iron. It "existed," of course, only in the heads of certain people and not in the "generally valid" reality. This system was defined still "more precisely" by Comrade Boyarkov in the *Vyestnik Metalista* (Petrograd, January, 1918), as "unfolded capitalism," which the working class must build "without employers." "Capitalism without capitalists." The want of clarity of the basic concepts led to this absurd form. We don't even want to mention the fact that bourgeois and opportunist literature is permeated by an even more serious muddle.

[102] Cf. N. Lenin, "Notes of a Publicist," in No. 9 of the *Communist International.*

[103] A fairly large number of "works" on socialism which have recently appeared circumvents this question. It is sufficient to cite as an example the work of Franz Eulenberg: *Arten und Stufen der Sozialisierung: Ein Gutachten,* Munich and Leipzig, 1920. On page 5 the author defines socialism as: "Socialization of the means of production; that includes the leadership of production and distribution for and by the sum total of the people." On page 6 he distinguishes, among others, the following "steps": under Rubric II: "Transfer of mature business into the hands of the whole; full socialization (nationalization)"; under Rubric III: "Participation by the whole on economic life in general: mixed economic businesses (state capitalism)." One can hardly manage to collect and write so much nonsense in so few "learned" lines as the honorable German investigator was able to. He sees the "sum total of the people" in the form of the state "in general," i.e. in such a state as does nowhere exist and also in an obviously capitalist state: on the one hand, socialism is "socialization" and nothing more; on the other hand, it is "Full-socialization," nationalization; the complete "socialization" is distinguished, according to Eulenburg, from the incomplete, as socialization from state capitalism, etc. And this is all arranged according to subjects, classified, and tabulated! Rudolf Goldscheid also does not show the slightest trace of understanding in his book, which is especially devoted to this theme. Cf. R. Goldscheid, *Staatssozialismus oder Staatskapitalismus. Ein Finanzsoziologischer Beitrag zur Lösung des Staatsschulden-Problems.* 4th and 5th edition, Vienna-Leipzig, 1917. In a highly interesting report by Otto Neurath (*Wesen und Wege der Sozialisierung*) the author attempts to evade the essence of the question by stating that the question as to which *means of power* are necessary for socialization is of no interest to him. However, he approaches the correct formulation of the question and is infinitely further than the learned and coquettish babbler Sombart. Cf., e.g., such lines: "Socialization presupposes that an *economic plan* is realized by some kind of decisive central authority. Such an *administrative economy* does not have to be of socialist nature; for instance, it can secure better conditions of life for a privileged group

of human beings; in Sparta a type of administrative economy secured for the Spartans the fruits of the labor of the Helots. . . . We call that person a socialist who advocates an *administrative economy* with *socialist distribution.*" (p. 4, emphasis by the author.) However, elimination of the question of the "means of power," i.e. of the class struggle and the classes, makes the entire formulation nebulous and vague.

L 199

[104] Incidentally: all "accusations" made by the petit bourgeoisie of the Social Democracy against the Communist Party are based on the misunderstanding of this situation. At best, these gentlemen protest against the "blockhead morality" and effect in this way a principal "equalization" of Communism and capitalist barbarism. As a matter of fact, can a "democrat" deny the "equal right of existence" of the wolf and of the sheep? That would certainly be contrary to divine justice.

L 200

[105] For the international opportunistic ideology, the fact is characteristic that this term is used as a substitute for "expropriation of the expropriators" and "confiscation." This happens so that one can more easily speak of "socialization" in connection with the ominous "totality," i.e. so that one can also count the measures of the state power of capital as part of "socialization." See especially the works of Edmund Fischer.

L 201

[106] Otto Bauer in his brochure, *Der Weg zum Sozialismus,* contrasts Socialization to Nationalization and sees in the first a combination of the organs from representatives of the workers, employees, and officials, on the one hand, and of the consumers, on the other hand, and of the state as a neutral quantity, on the third hand; the factories are to be leased, along with other measures, to agricultural cooperatives (i.e. to syndicates). The question of dictatorship is not correctly formulated; the state is a "democracy in general." This absolutely bourgeois point of view finds a much stronger expression in W. Rathenau, where the "Socialization" is carried out so that production is concentrated in the hands of capitalist professional groups. Concerning this "socialization theory," Dr. Karl Tyszka correctly remarks (*loc. cit.,* p. 25) that such a conception means the rebirth of medieval guilds. Prof. Tyszka himself, however, reveals not the slightest understanding of the class content of socialization. In Hermann Beck (*Sozialisierung als organisatorische Aufgabe*), the subjects of the socialization process are also the "interest-associations of employers." (p. 51.) In the conference of German engineers, Dr. Prange designates such a structure as "ennobled capitalism" and thereby turned up the cards. E. Fischer (*Vom Privatkapitalismus zum Sozialismus*), the classical model of Social Democratic cretins, plays the entire time with the concept of "Nationalization" and "Socialization," by turning them into two different meanings, and on the basis of this feat arrives at the brilliant result that "Socialization" has long been with us. Prof. Oppenheimer, who excellently understands the issue at hand, defends the capitalist position with the help of the theory of immaturity. For him, everyone who now aims at "Socialization" is a "putschist," "Blanquist," etc.

194

FOOTNOTES

[107] The latter term is of course not completely exact. First, it confuses the "nation" (the "totality") with the state, i.e. with the organization of the ruling class. Second, it bears the stamp of the age of national states. We maintain this term because it has come into use, although there exist no logical reasons for this.

L 202

[108] On the misunderstanding of this fact was based the illusion of so-called "municipal socialism." Certainly, in the process of the disintegration of capitalism and of the revolution, the seizure of power of individual districts by the proletariat and a proletarian "municipalization" under the state power of capital can occur through unorganized actions. But every reader will comprehend that this is a category of a completely different order. In the text we are speaking of relatively stable social systems.

[109] Cf. N. Lenin: Speech at the Ninth Congress of the Russian Communist Party.

[110] Cf., e.g., Frederick Winslow Taylor (*Principles of Scientific Management*).

[111] Therefore Otto Neurath is correct when he says that the "Ausschüsse" ("committees" or "councils") are scarcely usable for purely business founctions of production (also the same in F. Eulenberg, *loc. cit.*). Still, these "critics" absolutely do not understand, or act as if they do not understand, the social and socially *necessary* meaning of these transition forms. The question is correctly posed by Engineer Hermann Beck, *loc. cit.*

[112] If one understands under militia an *ideal* militia, where all its functions are voluntarily carried out in a manner similar to members of an orchestra who obey the baton, then one can apply Engels' words to it: "Only a society based on and educated in communism can approach closely to the militia system, and even then it will not completely achieve it." (Quoted according to Franz Mehring, *Karl Marx*, New York, 1935, p. 329.)

[113] Actually, the term "militarization," etc. is here totally inapplicable because the military organization of the proletarian state as well as the military character of the organization of industry has a completely different meaning. "Red militarism" is a downright barbaric word combination. But incorrectness of expression and custom of language force us to use the word "militarization" here.

L 203

[114] Therefore, e.g., the resolutions of the Ninth Congress of the Russian Communist Party, which were completely correct for the corresponding period of the existence of the Russian Soviet Republic, are absolutely unusable for the *chronologically* same moment in other countries. We cannot here speak extensively about the general system of administration, and we refer those who are interested to the following sources: *Protocol of the Ninth Congress of the Russian Communist Party;* the

newspaper *Ekonomitshiskaya Shisn* for the second half of March and the first half of April, 1920; *Protocol of the Third Congress of Trade Unions.*

[115] In Russia, Comrade Trotsky first emphasized this thought. It is well formulated by Hermann Beck: "An assembly of many people cannot make decisions, least of all on economic life with its complex connections and with the importance of every resolution. First of all, it must be said that it is not the duty of the shop steward to continually interfere in the course of the technological and economic factory administration, no more than a parliament can meddle in the routine business of the state administration. The administration of an enterprise also cannot be led by committees and councils; it must be directed by responsible, independently acting individual personalities who are trained as specialists. . . . The significance of all these collective organs can only be that they determine the factory constitution as well as the direction and spirit of the production achievement, and continually supervise the management of the factory leadership. . . . Also a second important function of the committees and councils is that of a mechanism for selection." (*Sozialisierung als organisatorische Aufgabe*, p. 52.) And in another place: "Only stubbornness can deny that shop steward and workers council are the most valuable new creations of political organization, although they are largely still unfruitful gossip clubs. . . . One must take care not to overlook the genuine essence of a form of organization because of the immaturity of its first phase of development." ("Eröffnungsansprache," p. 8.) Notwithstanding the last remark, Beck himself does not by far grasp the specific characteristics of the transformation process. Thus his organizational plans which, in terms of their structure, are absolutely unusable for that very period for which their author himself intended them.

[116] This chapter was composed on the basis of sketches which were made by my friend, Comrade J. Pyatakov. We intended to write this work in common. But to my deepest regret, practical duties diverted Comrade Pyatakov from this work and thwarted the mutual plan. I had to partly abridge this chapter, partly supplement and correspondingly revise the remaining part of the book. In many places the text of Comrade Pyatakov has remained unaltered. But even in the altered parts, the basic thoughts are his.

[117]. Marx, *Capital*, I, *loc. cit.*, p. 8.

[118] From this does not follow, of course, that one should not evaluate the empirical material. On the contrary. For "the method of advancing from the abstract to the concrete is but a way of thinking by which the concrete is grasped and is reproduced in our mind as a concrete." (Marx, *A Contribution to the Critique of Political Economy*, "Introduction," Chicago, 1904, pp. 293-4.) Cf. also N. Bukharin, *The Political Economy of the Leisure Class.*

196

FOOTNOTES

[119] This also makes itself obvious in the condition of our practical economic literature. As an example, we take an issue of the serious journal, *Narodnoye Khosyaistvo* (No. 5, 1919). Looking there at the article by I. D. Michalov, "The Condition of Railroad Transport," we find figures on the gross revenue, the "costs of exploitation," the "costs of maintenance of personnel," "the costs of exploitation per verst," and finally "net gains or deficit." All quoted figures show the sums in *roubles* and make the *comparison* for 1910-1918 and even for the first half of 1919. Finally the author painstakingly and persistently calculates the "flat cost"—likewise in roubles—of a pud in 1913, 14, 15, 16, 17, and 1918. By employing these arithmetic exercises, he draws the conclusion: "The flat cost of transport has therefore risen in the four years over five times as much." What significance do all these calculations have? The so-called "rouble rate of exchange" makes just such astonishing jumps as commodity in the chapter on fetishism in Marx's *Capital* or the table-turning by the spiritualists. Can we use the rouble as a unit of measure? This is one side of the question. What do these figures signify when the regulating role of the market disappears? The market, however, has not entirely disappeared; *in part* there exists a "free market" and "free prices"; in part "ceiling prices," and in part one receives food "free." But even that does not suffice. What do these numbers signify when many objects *cannot be attained at all* in excess, i.e. when the money-quantity becomes absolutely meaningless? All these questions do not once enter the head of the author of this article. And this is no isolated instance. This is a *typical* example of the characteristic vulgarization of our days.

[120] Marx, *Contribution to the Critique* . . ., "Introduction," *loc. cit.*, p. 268.

[121] Marx, *Letters to Dr. Kugelmann*, New York, 1934, p. 73 (letter dated July 11, 1868.)

[122] *Capital*, Vol. I.

[123] Herein exists the strongest revolutionary side of Marxist dialectics: "When the inner connection is grasped, all theoretical belief in the permanent necessity of existing conditions breaks down before their practical collapse." (*Letters to Dr. Kugelmann, loc. cit.*, p. 74.)

[124] Marx, *The Poverty of Philosophy.*

[125] On these methodological principles, cf. our work: *The Political Economy of the Leisure Class.*

[126] Cf. Engels' polemic against Rodbertus in the introduction to Marx's *Poverty of Philosophy.*

[127] *Letters to Kugelmann, loc. cit.*, pp. 73-74.

[128] We refer to the following highly interesting passage in *Capital* (Vol. I, pp. 354-6): "But what is it that forms the bond between the

independent labours of the cattle-breeder, the tanner, and the shoe-maker? It is the fact that their respective products are commodities. . . . It is only the common product of all the detail labourers that becomes a commodity. . . . Division of labour in society implies their [the means of production] dispersion among many independent producers of com-modities. While within the workshop, the iron law of proportionality subjects definite numbers of workmen to definite functions, in the society outside the workshop, chance and caprice have full play in distributing the producers and their means of production among the various branches of industry. *The different spheres of production, it is true, constantly tend to an equilibrium:* for, on the one hand, while each producer of a commodity is bound to produce a use-value, to satisfy a particular social want, and while the extent of these wants differs quantitatively, still there exists an inner relation which settles their proportions into a regular system, and that system one of spontaneous growth; and, on the other hand, the *law of the value of commodities* ultimately determines how much of its disposable working-time society can expend on each par-ticular class of commodities. But this constant tendency to equilibrium, of the various spheres of production, is exercised, only in he shape of *a reaction against the constant upsetting of the equilibrium.* The *a priori* system on which the division of labour, within the workshop, is regularly carried out, becomes in the division of labour within the society, an *a posteriori*, nature-imposed necessity, controlling the lawless caprice of the producers, and perceptible in the barometrical fluctuations of the market-prices." In these words lies *in nuce* the entire Marxist theory of the commodity economy, and here we see the role that the implicitly presupposed principle of equilibrium plays in the entire examination. It is interesting to note how Marx himself—*en passant*—characterizes his scientific method: "In reality, supply and demand never coincide. . . . But political economy assumes that supply and demand coincide with one another. Why? To be able to study phenomena in their fundamental relations, in the form corresponding to their conception, that is, to study them independent of the appearances caused by the movement of sup-ply and demand." (*Capital,* Vol. III, pp. 189-190.) That means to ob-serve the social economy in the condition of equilibrium.

[129] Marx, *The Poverty of Philosophy,* p. 93. There we also find another formulation of the same thought: "Economic categories are only the theoretical expressions, the abstractions of the social relations of produc-tion." (ibidem, p. 92.)

[130] Marx distinguishes (*Contribution to the Critique,* "Introduction,"), in addition to the production relations, derived production relations. The talk is also about the appearance of the latter.

[131] Marx, *Capital,* Vol. I, p. 714.

[132] Thus the works of E. Dühring; of subsequent authors: Gumplowicz; of more recent ones: Franz Oppenheimer.

FOOTNOTES

133 Cf. on this Engels, *Anti-Dühring*. Also Engels, *Force and Economy*.

134 Marx, *Capital*, Vol. I, p. 751.

135 Kautsky, Bauer, and *tutti quanti* reject force with indignation and revulsion, no matter what its source. The creators of scientific communism had a different attitude towards this question. Thus Engels, e.g. wrote about Dühring: "That force, however, plays another role in history, a revolutionary role . . . of this there is not a word in Herr Dühring. It is only with sighs and groans (hear! hear! N. B.) that he admits the possibility that force will perhaps be necessary for the overthrow of the economic system of exploitation—unfortunately, because all use of force, forthooth, demoralizes the person who uses it. . . . And this persons' mode of thought—lifeless, insipid and impotent—claims to impose itself on the most revolutionary party which history has known!" (Engels, *Herr Eugen Dühring's Revolution in Science*, New York, 1935, pp. 209-10.) One must recollect at Kautsky's observations on "beastiality" and "humanity" the brilliant lines of Engels on the "true socialists." "Some humanity," as one says today, some "realization" of this humanity, or more correctly of the monstrosity, very little about the sufferings of the proletariat, the organization of labor, the planting of the inevitable but boring organizations to raise the lower classes of the people. And besides this, boundless ignorance about questions of the actual social life. That is the content of their entire literature, which thanks to the "absolute objectivity" of thinking loses the last remnants of energy and activity. And with this boring stuff one intends to revolutionize Germany, to rouse the proletariat, and to create in the masses the ability to think and to act. These Philistinian cowardly traits of the "true socialists" were also typical of internal party relations. "It is characteristic of these old women," Marx thought, "that they are always striving to gloss over and whitewash all real party disputes." (Quoted according to Mehring, *loc. cit.*, p. 142.) Is that not the true paragon of the "objective," "neutral," "independent theorist?" | L 204

136 *The Communist Manifesto*, II: "Proletarians and Communists."

137 Therefore the conception of Kautsky and his like is nonsensical, when they conceive of the revolution as similar to parliamentary voting, where an arithmetic quantity (half of the population plus 1) is decisive. Cf. Lenin, "The elections to the Constitutional Assembly and the Dictatorship of the Proletariat."

138 The "atoning nobleman" is the figure from the Narodniki period of the Russian liberation movement, when sons and daughters from feudal families "went to the people" out of pure idealism. Cf. e.g., Turgenjev's *Virgin Soil*.

139 A Communist who has committed a crime is much more strictly punished in Soviet Russia at the initiative of the party than a "simple mortal." | L 205

[140] The law of the Russian Mensheviks against compulsion in the era of the proletarian dictatorship is just the same as the cry of the capitalists against the rape of "freedom to work" by the unions, who set up pickets during a strike and prevent the capitalists from using strikebreakers. As is well known, the capitalist clique commits the most malicious acts under the very slogan of "protection of the freedom to work."

[141] Opposed views on the stability of the economic organisms were set forth by some ideologists of economic backwardness. Thus, e.g., in the well-known book of General Hulewitsch on war and political economy. On the other hand, the young Russian imperialists also scented *the danger de pur sang* (of course within the limited framework of "mischief" which did not go beyond capitalism). Cf., e.g., the article by P. Struve in the omnibus edition, *Great Russia* (Russian), also S. Prokopovitch, *War and Political Economy* (Russian).

[142] It is self-evident that the equality of the remaining conditions is presupposed here. The simple, mechanical preponderance of powers can also be on the side of the backwards groups if they represent a quantitatively greater sum.

[143] As a vulgar "specimen" of the opposite point of view, the work of the Narodnik (leftist social revolutionary) W. Trutovski will serve: *The Transition Period* (Russian).

[144] A brilliant analysis of the revolutionary situation and its models is found in Lenin's work, *"Left-Wing" Communism—An Infantile Disorder.*

[145] John Keynes writes in his book (*The Economic Consequences of the Peace*, London, 1919): "The Treaty includes no provisions for the economic rehabilitation of Europe,—nothing to make the defeated Central Empires into good neighbors, nothing to stabilize the new States of Europe, nothing to reclaim Russia; nor does it promote in any way a compact of economic solidarity among the Allies themselves; nor arrangement was reached at Paris for restoring the disordered finances of France and Italy, or to adjust the systems of the Old World and the New" (p. 211). Keynes characterizes the situation as follows: "The significant features of the immediate situation can be grouped under the heads: first, the absolute falling-off, for the time being, in Europe's internal productivity; second, the breakdown of transport and exchange by means of which its products could be conveyed where they were most wanted; and third, the inability of Europe to purchase its usual supplies from overseas" (p. 216). Keynes speaks of the threatening social catastrophe and of the mood of the ruling classes. The collapse of the imperialist system drives into the imperialists the love for a community of interests. Thus Roedder (*loc. cit.*, p. 50) says: "Just as bricks in a large structure mutually support each other, are laid against and protect each other, so in living together and in the mutual forward efforts of nations, one rests on the next. But if one brick is worn, it must be replaced in

200

good time with a better one so that no danger develops for the entire structure," etc. All these dismal observations end with the tragic: "To be or not to be—that is the question." For the *capitalist* system, history answers with a decisive No.

[146] In these cases, which as one can easily see may in no way be taken as typical, a total disintegration of the apparatus does not occur, as it appears in the typical case of social transformation. | L 208

[147] Prof. C. Ballod believes in his naiveté that we Russian Communists think that Communism is possible at the level of the proletarian dictatorship, and he makes a whole series of the most ridiculous accusations against us, which reveal his own ignorance. Cf. C. Ballod, "Kommunismus und Sozialismus," *Der Sozialist (Sozialistische Auslandspolitik)* No. 34, Aug. 23, 1919.

AFTERWORD TO THE GERMAN EDITION

Since this book was written, some time has elapsed. Since then in Russia the so-called "new direction in economic policy" has been adopted, which for the first time brought socialized industry, petit-bourgeois economy, private-capitalist business, and the "mixed" enterprises into correct economic relation to each other. This specifically *Russian* change, the deepest precondition of which is the peasant-agrarian character of the country, caused some of my ingenious critics to remark that I must rewrite my work from the beginning. This view rests on the total illiteracy of these clever ones, who in their sacred simplicity do not grasp the difference between an abstract examination, which depicts things and processes in their "ideal cross-cut"—according to the expression by Marx— and the empirical reality, which is always and under all circumstances infinitely more complicated than its abstract representation. I have not written an economic *history* of Soviet Russia but rather a general theory of the transition period, for which the powers of comprehension of the journalists *par excellence* and of the narrow "practical men," who are unable to comprehend the general problems, are no match. But I, of course, am not responsible for their shortcomings.

The same error is basically at the bottom of tactical theory as well—the "offensive under all circumstances"— which is popular in some circles of our German comrades

202

and which wants to rely on my work for its justification. It is meanwhile self-evident that the inference for concrete action can no more be derived from my work than, say, from the "theory of impoverishment."

It is possible that the German edition of the book will evoke in our enemies (also in the purely bourgeois critics and the so-called Social Democrats, who now, with unheard-of audacity want to eliminate all essential elements of Marxist theory) the feeling of a certain moral satisfaction, for I openly admit the, objectively speaking, inevitably destructive effect of the revolution as such. From a purely human point of view, I am glad that I can grant these people this pleasure. And even more so, as the pessimistic impression of "healthy capitalism" will lead the Social Democracy to a return to Kant and to Vorländer as the official party philosophers, but will lead the bourgeoisie to a turning away from Kant and towards the Indian fakirs (Keyserling) in order to seek consolation at the banks of the Ganges. The revolutionary workers, however, will understand very well that as soon as the "capitalist veil is lifted" (Marx), an idyllic course of development as seen by Cunow cannot possibly be demanded. As far as laughter is concerned, however, it is still said that "he laughs best who laughs last."

Moscow, December, 1921

N. Bukharin

Chart I (to chapter I)

A. World economy in the epoche
of industry-capitalism

B. World economy in the epoche
of finance-capitalism

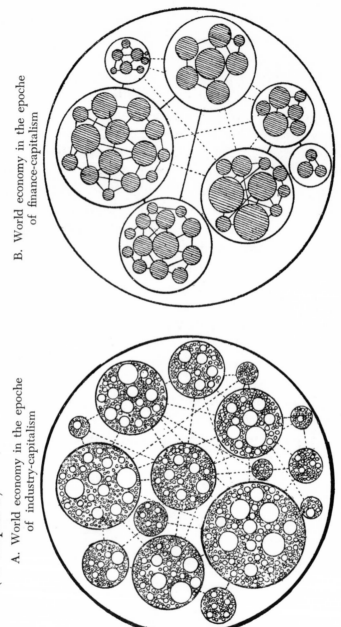

The small circles and dots designate the enterprises within the un-organized "national" economies.—Dotted lines show the connections between the latter which have mainly the form of market exchange.

The small circles are the banks, trusts and syndicates, organically connected among themselves to a system which builds the state-capitalistic trust.—Dotted lines show the less closely connections between the state-capitalistic trusts.—Solid rules mean the close associations, mainly their partnerships and financing.

Chart II (to chapter III)

System of State-Capitalism

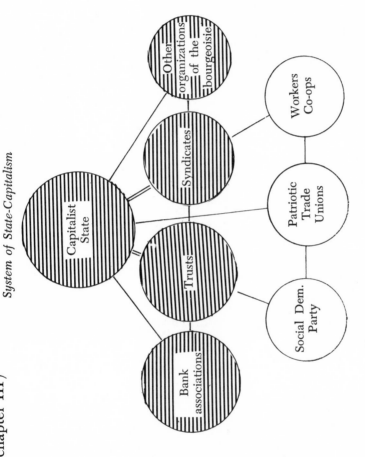

Chart III (to chapter III)

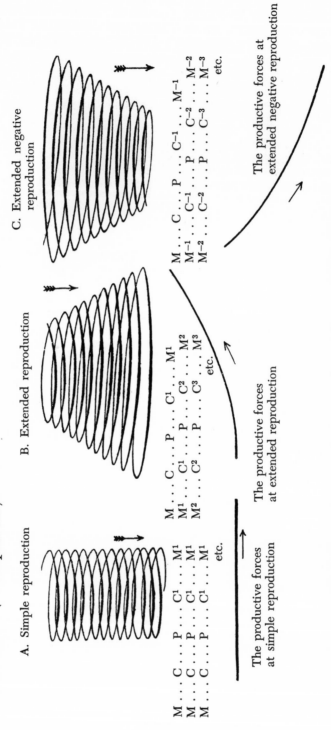

A. Simple reproduction

M . . . . C . . . . P . . . . C¹ . . . . M¹
M . . . . C . . . . P . . . . C¹ . . . . M¹
M . . . . C . . . . P . . . . C¹ . . . . M¹
etc.

The productive forces
at simple reproduction

B. Extended reproduction

M . . . . C . . . . P . . . . C¹ . . . . M¹
M¹ . . . . C¹ . . . . P . . . . C² . . . . M²
M² . . . . C² . . . . P . . . . C³ . . . . M³
etc.

The productive forces
at extended reproduction

C. Extended negative
reproduction

M . . . . C . . . . P . . . . C⁻¹ . . . . M⁻¹
M⁻¹ . . . . C⁻¹ . . . . P . . . . C⁻² . . . . M⁻²
M⁻² . . . . C⁻² . . . . P . . . . C⁻³ . . . . M⁻³
etc.

The productive forces at
extended negative reproduction

For reasons of simplification the un-productive consumption is always disregarded—except group A.

Chart IV (to chapter IV)

State-capitalism and the system of proletarian dictatorship

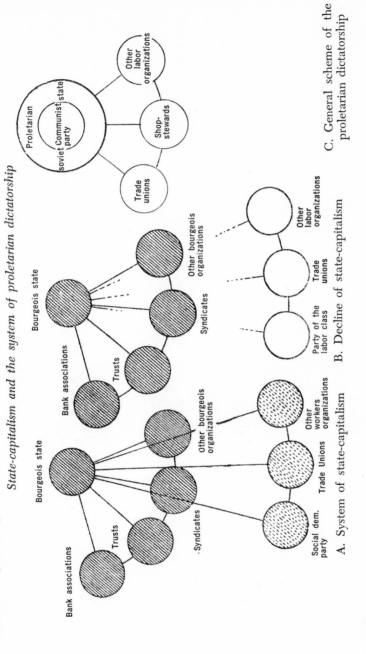

A. System of state-capitalism

B. Decline of state-capitalism

C. General scheme of the proletarian dictatorship

Chart V (to chapters III and IV)

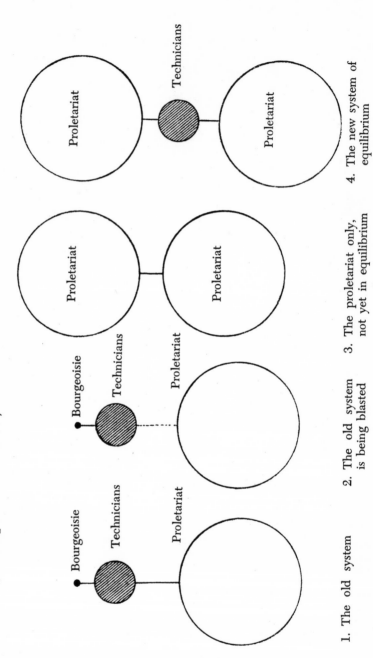

1. The old system

2. The old system is being blasted

3. The proletariat only, not yet in equilibrium

4. The new system of equilibrium

Chart VI (to chapter III)

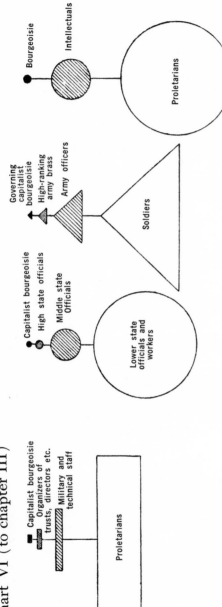

The anarchy of production in capitalist society

The hierarchic state apparatus of the bourgeoisie

The military organization of the bourgeois state

General scheme of capitalist relationships

Chart VII (to chapter V)

City and Country in the Transformation Process

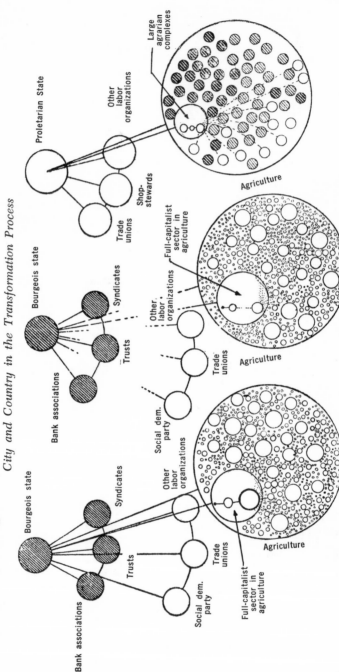

A. State-capitalistic system   B. Decline of the state-capitalistic system   C. System of the proletarian dictatorship

LENIN'S REMARKS

to *"The Economics of the Transformation Period"*

> "Bukharin is the most valuable and most important
> theoretician of the Party but . . . I believe he never
> completely understood dialectics."
>
> —Lenin's Testament, written
> December 25, 1922.

Shortly after Bukharin was officially classified as the leader of the *Primiryaniye* ("Reconciliation"), the Lenin Institute reproduced (in "Lenin Sbornik," Vol. XI, 1929) the notations Lenin had made in pencil on various margins, right and left, above and below, in his copy of the *Economics of the Transformation Period*. In addition appeared a general review of Bukharin's book, written by Lenin on May 31, 1920 for the newly created Communist Academy of which this book had been its first publication.

Obviously used by the Stalin party leadership to degrade Bukharin's eminent position as the theoretician of the party, Lenin's critic nevertheless enhanced the importance of Bukharin's book. Although with reservations of a methological nature and critical hints about terminology (and exposing minor errors which he advised to be corrected in a popularized edition of the book), Lenin agrees enthusiastically with Bukharin about all fundamental problems of the economics of the revolutionary state.

Lenin wrote these remarks to this book at the end of the same month he finished his epoch making pamphlet, *Left-Wing Communism—an Infantile Disorder*, which was written under the influence of his preparations for the economic reconstruction program, officially announced by Lenin only a year later under the title "NEP." The abandonment of most of the principal economic features which according to Bukharin's book are fundamental for

Thanks are due to Stephen F. Cohen for providing a Xerox-copy of the Russian texts of Lenin's remarks. Dr. Cohen is the author of a larger study on Bukharin, to be published by Alfred A. Knopf in 1972.

211

the proletarian revolution in its transition to socialism, especially the striking restoration of the wage system, seemed to Lenin not to be in conflict with this book's theoretical content, because NEP was intended as a temporary measure, caused only or mainly by the defeats of all revolutionary attempts in postwar Europe.

It is interesting that though knowing Lenin's remarks and in spite of the decisive turn towards NEP about which Bukharin delivered the official report before the Third World Congress on July 8, 1921, Bukharin authorized in December 1921 the German edition of this book, without any change, well aware that the same German and other European communists against whom Lenin had directed his sharp critic of "Left-Wing Communism" saw in Bukharin's book a justification of their "Theory of Offensive Under All Conditions." In fact, Bukharin's book became the economic-theoretical approval of the theory of Revolution in Permanence *versus* the theory of "Socialism in One Country."

Up until the introduction of the Five-year-plan, in 1928, which coincided with Bukharin's downfall as the leader of the Comintern, *Economics of the Transformation Period* was considered as an achievement of Bolshevik theory next in importance to Lenin's *State and Revolution.*   P.M.B.

LENIN'S MARGINAL REMARKS

L 1) What is this??? "General"? à la Spencer?

L 2) *Indicating "changing" within a box, Lenin remarks*: Well, thank God: not "transformation," and not in general, but recognized for what it is!!

L 3) *Indicating "subject" within a box, Lenin puts in the margin two question marks and says*: "Important," than class!

L 4) *Indicating "vices" within a box, Lenin sets a question mark in the margin.*

L 5) *Indicating "Promethus" within a box, Lenin remarks*: Ugh!!

L 6) Only the "theory of knowledge" ?? And not reflecting the objective world? "Shameful" . . . agnosticism!

L 7) Two errors: 1) a determined step backwards compared to Engels; 2) Commodity production is also "organized" economy. *Underlining the words "sociological introduction," Lenin remarks*: Ugh!

212

L 8) Wrong. Even in pure communism though would be the ratio I v + s to II c?* And accumulation?

L 9) Not only!

L 10) Precisely *not* for this reason. *Lenin also underlines the words "completely irrelevant" and "relatively unimportant."*

L 11) *Underlining "entire world," Lenin says:* Not everywhere.

L 12) *Boxing-in "subjects" and "state-capitalist trusts," Lenin remarks:* Not only.

L 13) Has not "abrogated."

L 14) *Underlining the words "social," "still means" and "enterprises," Lenin sets a question mark in the margin.*

L 15) Ugh! A play with definitions. *Lenin underlines and questions the words "rational organization" and "anarchy."*

L 16) *Lenin boxes-in the word "power," and underlines with a wavy rule the words "therefore" and "here" and remarks:* ? Powerful ? ("important") not "therefore" and not "here." Colonies existed both before imperialism and even before industrial capitalism.

L 17) A play with analogies. *Underlining "decline of independent states," Lenin remarks:* Sometimes the *creation* of independent states means the strengthening of imperialism.

L 18) *Underlining "anarchic" and boxing-in "as," Lenin remarks:* Why and under what conditions this "as"??!?

L 19) "However . . ." is not good.

L 20) Very good!

L 21) "Constitutive marks of all social appearances"—not good!

L 22) Ugh! Ugh! This is just as if a chemist on page 25 of a chemistry text spoke of the "natural historical point of view." And what point of view *would oppose* it?

L 23) *Underlining "war . . . sociological," Lenin remarks:* Psychological? Zu einfach und ungenau.

L 24) Not only.

L 25) But sometimes war is a "means" (an unsuitable word) of the *disintegration* of the regime.

L 26) Ugh! Oh! Help! totale Konfusion hervorgerufen durch zu grosse Liebe des Verfassers Begriffsspiel zu üben und dasselbe

---

* Note by the publisher of the English edition: Lenin uses here Marx's formula of Simple Reproduction (Cf. *Capital* II, pp. 402 ff.) which is: I (v + s) *versus* II c.

für "Soziologie" zu erklären . . .

L 27) *Throughout this whole chapter, Lenin boxes-in the word "system," obviously in disagreement.*

L 28) Ugh! Help!

L 29) *Boxing-in the words "above all" and adding a question mark, Lenin says*: Classes represent by themselves above all "groups of persons" (vaguely phrased) who are distinguished by their position in the social structure of production and those who are distinguished in that one group can take on the work of another group.

L 30) Extremely unclear. Antagonism and contradiction are not at all the same thing. The former disappears, the latter remains under socialism.

L 31) Ugh!

L 32) Help!

L 33) Ein bischen zu viel. Qui prouve trop . . . The next phrase does not follow from "on the contrary."

L 34) This is true.

L 35) Very good and it would have been still better to say it more simply instead of "mode of connection."

L 36) Ugh!

L 37) This depends upon whether the proletariat "on the basis of class struggle" (a pitty! So much for "sociology"! So much for organizational science!) would be able to bring about the total downfall.

L 38) Well! Thank God! Finally, human language instead of "organizational" gibberish! All is well that ends well. *Lenin underlines "the centralization of the means of production and the socialization of labor" and adds in the margin*: 1) and 2).

L 39) Ugh! Again! Perhaps it could have been "social" and not organizational point of view?

L 40) Is broken into pieces.

L 41) Why? In the first (*place*)?

L 42) Dialectical process. Precisely! And not as scholastic à la Bogdanov. The author places himself side by side (and in 2 places) with Bogdanov's Begriffsscholastik. They can not be placed side by side: either—or.

L 43) Very true!

L 44) True!

L 45) "Impossibility" demonstrates only the practical. The author does not consider the dialectic relationships of theory and practice.

L 46) NB true! Now this is here getting nearer to dialectics.

L 47) Very true!

L 48) *Lenin underlines with a wavy rule the word "transforma-tion" and also "social labor," to the latter he remarks*: Not this word.

L 49) "My" Begriffsscholastik by Bogdanov is the worst enemy of "mine."

L 50) Not this word.

L 51) *Boxing-in "formally," Lenin installs in the margin*: ??

L 52) *Boxing-in "regrouping" and underlining "if the relations of production," Lenin installs in the margin*: ?? *He also underlines the word "Social-caste."*

L 53) Why is that?

L 54) *Lenin underlines the whole paragraph and remarks in the margin*: Sehr gut!

L 55) Not that word. Division (from). *Lenin critisizes that Bu-kharin translates Marx's word "Scheidung" with "razgrantchemiye" which means "bordering-off." Engels' authorized English edition of* Capital, *as used in the present book, translates the word with "separ-ation." Lenin's "division from" is undoubtedly correct. Lenin also boxes-in, obviously critically, "summed up" (zusammenfasst") which Bukharin wrongly translates with "postroyena" = built-on.*

L 56) Why not profitability without quotation marks?

L 57) Very good.

L 58) *Underlining "organizational," Lenin remarks*: The author obviously wants to say: "The process of socialization" but his word (as opposed to the other word) does not express this thought.

L 59) Black market.

L 60) Add: the third in place of the first in importance.

L 61) Very true!

L 62) Add: in Western Europe, not in Russia (and in Western Europe only until the victory of the proletariat).

L 63) Inevitable with time.

L 64) He should have said: Between the *socialist* tendencies of the proletariat and the commodity oriented capitalistic tendency of the peasantry. To put in the word organizing is a theoretical inaccuracy, a step back from Karl Marx towards Louis Blanc.

L 65) *Boxing-in "formula," Lenin says*: Ha-ha-ha!! An atrociously wrong term! The wiser the more inexact theoretically.

L 66) *Underlining "founded," Lenin writes in the margin*: necessary.

L 67) Very good.

L 68) Not only formally.

L 69) Not only formally.

L 70) Precisely!

L 71) True, and better than "anarchy."

L 72) Inaccurate to say and think (as frequently the author does) that "complete decomposition" is "necessary" for the trusts.

L 73) This terminology is a deliberate substitution of classes by the formation of groups and therefore is it not a step backwards towards "sociology" in quotation marks?

L 74) To relate is not to identify.

L 75) *Underlining with wavy rule "personal" and with two straight rules "correspondingly," Lenin remarks*: "Correspondingly" is not apparent here because "personal" (an inexact term) is not "technical".

L 76) This is better than on page 88 (*of the Russian edition— Lenin means the part he just criticized*).

L 77) Mathematics is worse than suspicious. It is useless.

L 78) *Triple underlining "we need a sociological definition of productive powers," Lenin remarks*: Ha-ha!

L 79) *Underling "war" and boxing-in "method," Lenin remarks*: Not in general, not every (war).

L 80) Not exactly.

L 81) America in 1870 compared with 1860 in its census.

L 82) True!

L 83) Compare Engels on "destruction" in his letter (1882) on Colonies (*The editors of "Leninskii Sbornik" mistakingly changed Lenin's reference in a special footnote, believing that it is a letter from the year 1892. In fact, Lenin's reference is correct. It is the letter to Kautsky, dated September 12, 1882 in which Engels says that "all kinds of destruction are naturally just inseparable from all revolutions."*) *

* Note by the publisher of this English edition: Beyond the great im-

216

L 84) Distorted and imprecise terminology, facilitating the conquest of state power by the class.

L 85) Ugh!! *Lenin refers especially to "socialist primitive accumulation"* and boxing-in "self," underlining "organization of the working masses."*

L 86) With the mobilization and with "socialization."

L 87) There should be more on this.

L 88) Perhaps a definition of state capitalism would be in order. A capitalism without stocks and trusts (and perhaps without monopolies). The author gives neither a concrete nor an economic judgment.

L 89) Completely true!

L 90) A bad definition. There is nothing indispensible in it. And "rationalization"—not always. "The domination of capital" and "antagonism" are one and the same. Already before state capitalism there was (and is) a dictatorship of the bourgeoisie.

L 91) This is a tautology.

L 92) True!

L 93) *Twice underlining the word "impossible," Lenin remarks*: An exaggeration. It is possible, for example, in two or three small states, if, at first, the workers are entirely victorious in the four or five largest and most progressive states.

L 94) *Boxing-in "socialist," Lenin remarks*: Hmm!!? (*Obviously, ironically about Bukharin's term "socialist dictatorship."*)

L 95) The author abuses the word "dialectic negation": it cannot

portance Lenin gave this letter by Engels for emphasizing Bukharin's dealings with the destruction of productive forces as a result of revolution, we want to quote Engels extensively: "Which social and political phases those countries (India, Algeria, Egypt etc.) will then (after revolution in Europe and North America) experience, till they also will achieve socialist organization, about that, I believe, we can today only construe some idle hypotheses. Only one thing is sure: The victorious proletariat cannot press any blessings upon other nations without undermining its own victory. Wherewith defensive wars of all kinds are naturally by no means excluded." *Marx-Engels Werke*, Berlin, 1967, Vol. 35, pp. 357-8.

* A term introduced at that time by Russian Marxists and also later frequently used by the "right"-wing Communist August Thalheimer in reasoning with Soviet policy in East-European countries after World War II. (Note by the publisher of this edition.)

be used if it has not been proven with facts first.

L 96) Nationally, not collectively.

L 97) ???? monstrous.

L 98) There is no contradiction here.

L 99) Exactly!

L 100) Precisely *not* this. Where? When? The author does not express himself clearly.

L 101) Exactly!

L 102) !? Not at all. He "justifies" the mixing of the "process" of the birth of a man with the "process" of his death!

L 103) Well said!

L 104) That is it exactly!

L 105) Exactly!

L 106) ? That does not happen. Profit also satisfies "social" needs. He should have said: Where the surplus product goes not to the propertied class, but to all workers and only to them.

L 107) True! Only the words "regime of persons" are not exact. Hat Nebenbedeutung. Not this word.

L 108) Here is the essence. The author ought to dwell more on the notion of (the working class as) "ruling class."

L 109) Very good!

L 110) Hmm, hmm!

L 111) *Lenin is underlining these words; apparently in approval.*

L 112) "Social system," "social formation"—all this is insufficiently concrete without an understanding of *class* and class society.

L 113) Dialectics includes the historical.

L 114) True. Compare with earlier inprecision.

L 115) Of approximate, rough (equilibrium), in large numbers, à la longue.

L 116) This is very good. But is it not more precise to speak about the "necessity of known proportionality" than about "the point of view equilibrium"? It is more precise and true since objectively first and second the door is half open for philosophical vacillation from materialism towards idealism.

L 117) Precisely!

L 118) The elements of disintegration are limited . . . ugh! . . . Why not simply "limits them"? Oh, academism! Oh, false classicism! Oh, Tretyakovski!

L 119) Not this word (*"consider"*). The mistake of "Bogdano-vistic" terminology stands out: *Subjectivism*, solipcism. The point does not lie in who "views" whom as "interesting," but in the fact that there is a dependence on human perception.

L 120) "The method transforms another tone." Bukharin adopts a *stupid* tone. There is no "tone" or "logic" here, only matter.

L 121) *Lenin boxes-in "on the whole" and installs in the margin a question mark.* (Material production) does not have a "point of view."

L 122) Untrue. Formerly the bourgeoisie "coerced" through the court, tax collectors, taxes etc. (Cf. Marx on France, not only on Russia). Now the *proletariat* coerces *more directly*. The author forgot "social-class" relations.

L 123) Not only "on the surface" and not only "of the phenom-ena."

L 124) It is a great relief to see in this phrase that the author, spoiled by the eclecticism of Bogdanov, the dialectical "point of view" is only one of many equally valid "points of view." Untrue!

L 125) *Here Lenin installs in the margin two question marks.*

L 126) 3 years (>) in Russia!

L 127) Precisely! But it is *always* relative.

L 128) From this here the *invalidity* of the phrase is clear: "The postulate of equilibrium is not apparent."

L 129) Now, this is precise, simple and clear, without preten-tious formulations of dialectical materialism. Quantum mutatus ab illo the eclecticism of Bukharin!

L 130) True!

L 131) Imprecise: It is not transformed into a "product" but something else. Etwa: in a product designed for social use and not through the market.

L 132) Les mots, qui hurlent de se voir accouplés.

L 133) True!

L 134) True! And well said, without pretense. It would be neces-sary to develop this (in detriment to the ten pages with "points of view.")

L 135) True!

L 136) Notabene "definition": delightful.

L 137) *Boxing-in "power," Lenin remarks*: Would it not be more precise to say "category" ?, "factor"? (Compulsion power is not good in Russian.) *

L 138) The author should have added:
1) statistical figures;
2) on their role in economics of the country;
3) on its ties with the mass of workers,
4) on its organization.

L 139) *Lenin underlines this sentence by Marx.*

L 140) Very good!

L 141) True!

L 142) True! *Lenin underlines twice the word "inevitably."*

L 143) The forces of the proletariat surrounding the dictatorship of the proletariat—it is impossible to say such a thing.

L 144) True! *Lenin underlines twice the words "gathered," "placed" and "fitted."*

L 145) True!

L 146) *Underlining the word "re-edication" twice, Lenin remarks:* C'est le mot.

L 147) In the process of being born.

L 148) *Underlining "even to the ruling class," Lenin remarks:* True!

L 149) Not in the "presupposing" thing (this is idealistic), but in the *material*: there is *no* compact uniformity.

L 150) *Twice underlining the words "primitive . . . error," Lenin says:* True!

L 151) Very good!

L 152) True!

L 153) There, precisely!

L 154) True!

L 155) True!

L 156) True!

L 157) *Encircling "more or less," Lenin writes in the margin:* Vigorously (not ⟩ or ⟨).

---

* Note by the publisher of this English edition: In the German original of *Capital* the word is "Potenz" which as a technical term in mathematics means "involvement" or in electricity "energy." Engel's authorized English translation which is here used, also uses "power" and can lead to inclarity.

L 158) *Underlining "vacillate constantly," Lenin remarks*: True!

L 159) True!

L 160) True!

L 161) Precisely!

L 162) Very good!

L 162a) *At the end of this chapter, this time not in the margin, Lenin writes*: This is an excellent chapter!

L 163) Inevitability of the 1914-18 war is due not only to this.

L 164) War of 1914-18, but not the war of 1911-12. The academic omits *differentian specificam*.

L 165) *Underlining "state" with a heavy wave and then underlining the next sentence, Lenin says*: True!

L 166) Precisely: Under monopolistic capitalism (the author in general forgets this quite frequently).

L 167) Notabene: Not finance-capitalistic organization, but the organization of capitalism into finance capital.

L 168) True!

L 169) *Underlining "weakest," Lenin remarks*: Untrue: with "average weakness." Without the granted height of capitalism it would not have happened.

L 170) True! He should have said: with the leaders of the working class.

L 171) True!

L 172) Risky: he should have said "not from the higher" and "not direct proportion."

L 173) Very good!

L 174) *Underlining "class," Lenin remarks*: Not that word.

L 175) *Boxing-in "purest" and underlining "shadings," Lenin remarks*: Not the *purest fiction*, but an impure form. The violation of "dialectical materialism" consists in the *logical* (not material) galloping through *several* concrete stages.

L 176) The author forgot that (1) imperialistic states grew out of national (states); (2) that "national" states are formed in colonies.

L 177) Exactly!

L 178) Very good!

L 179) Is it not just the contrary: at the beginning "further," then "later" and finally "first"?

L 180) Loria is quite another matter.

L 181) He should have specified: even the sensible bourgeoisie (Delbrück) understands this better than Kautsky, Otto Bauer and Co.

L 182) *Lenin underlines the words "permanent revolution," and installs two question marks in the margin.*

L 183) *Lenin writes in the margin:* NB (*which refers to his "Notabene" comment 2 in "Summa Summarum"*).

L 184) Marx said it more simply (without flourishes of terminology, systematics, and sociology) and he spoke more *accurately* about *socialization.* The author gives valuably *new facts,* but deteriorates, verballhornt the theory of Marx with "sociological" scholasticism.

L 185) Very good!

L 186) Not social.

L 187) Very true!

L 188) *Lenin underlines heavily parts of the quote from Capital:* "der über die Herrschaft auf dem Weltmarkt entscheiden soll," *and* "den Keim einer weit gewaltigen Krise in sich."

L 189) Not so much.

L 190) The terminology is simply wrong here. There are no classes which are not social. He should have said more simply and accurately (theoretically): he (Kautsky) forgot the *class struggle.*

L 191) *Boxing-in "sociologist," Lenin remarks:* Well, the "sociologist" Bukharin finally puts the word "sociologist" into ironic quotation marks! Bravo!

L 192) Ah, ah! What lack of understanding of the "social class" relationships—A book with untranslated quotations is barred from the workers!*

L 193) This is not to the point.

L 194) Page 94 (*of the Russian edition*). *Lenin underlines* "the destruction" *which was caused by the Civil war in America.*

L 195) Very good!

L 196) NB. This was forgotten by the author on pages 88-90 and following. *Lenin refers to the pagination in the Russian edition—In*

---

* Note by the publisher of this English edition: Bukharin quotes in the original languages only. Following the authorized German edition we give translations into English.

the present English edition see pp. 98-100.

L 197) True!

L 198) And extremely unfortunate. A childish game in its imitation of terms, used by adults.

L 199) Very good!

L 200) Very good!

L 201) True!

L 202) ??? This is not a merging but an *historical* fact. The author "forgot" that a typical state under capitalism is a national state (plus colony, but this does not pertain to the question).

L 203) Add: Anti-bourgeoisie ("social-democratic") pacifism.

L 204) Very good!

L 205) ? He should have said: He receives on the initiative of the party.

L 206) True!

L 207) Très bien!

L 208) True!

Summa summarum: A spoonful of tar in a barrel of honey

Comment 2 on page 33 (Lenin refers to footnote 28 of the present English edition): Naively, almost childishly naively, Bukharin "took terms" "after the significant book" in the sense in which they are used by Comrade A. Bogdanov—————and did not think that the terms and their meanings had been "consolidated" (I hope the academic author forgives this funny term) by Bogdanov in his philosophy, a philosophy of idealism and eclecticism. Therefore quite frequently, too frequently in fact, the author falls into a contradiction with dialectical materialism (i.e. Marxism), scholasticism of terms (agnostic, Hume-Kantian, along a philosophical basis) into idealism ("logic," "point of view" etc. . . .) unaware of their derivation from *matter*, from objective reality etc. From this point on follows a line of *theoretical* inaccuracies (to what relates *"general theory"*?), of learned arguments and well-meaning academic stupidities. This book would be quite excellent if the author would discard the subtitle ("General Theory") in a second edition, discard pp. 20 to 30* of his scholasticism, his unconsciously idealistic

* Note to this English edition: Lenin means especially chapter Three and Four.

223

(in the philosophical sense) and eclectic exercises in terminology, and replace these pp. 20 to 30 with *facts* (from the rich economic literature which he quotes). Then the book would begin to *recover* from its bloated illness, become trim, strengthen its bones, decrease its anti-Marxist fat and in this way would firmly "consolidate" (Ha-ha!) the excellent conclusion of the book.

When the author personally gets his facts confused—he shows himself to be nicely and happily unpedantic. But when he blindly reflects Bogdanov's "terminology" (it is not at all a question of terms, but of philosophical errors) as he does at the beginning of the book, for the sake of importance, of academism, his thinking is frequently turned upside down so that he can later turn it about and assert himself—this is definitely irrelevant pedanticism.

Might we hope that in the second edition etc., etc.

On pages 131 and 133 the difference between Marxism and "Bogdanovism" is clearly "overemphasized."

May 31, 1920.

Recensio academica: The superior qualities of this excellent book put several disqualifications to the test, in so far as they are limited by circumstance, in the first place, that the author does not sufficiently consolidate his postulates with solid, yet brief, factual material, which would give him a command of the literature.

A consolidated body of fact would save this book from defects of "sociological aspects" or, more accurately, of philosophical aspects. But in the second place the author views the economic processes insufficiently concrete *in actu*, frequently lapsing into what we call "terminus technicus"—"Begriffsscholastik" and not taking into account that many unsuccessful formulations and terms rooted in philosophy falling under the heading of "Grundgedanken" under the line idealismi philosophici seu agnosticismi: (recht oft unbesehen und unkritisch von anderen übernommen), this is not materialismi. Let us express our hope that this small defect will disappear in subsequent editions which are indispensible to our reading public and which serve the great honor of the academy; we congratulate the academy on the splendid work of its member.

May 31, 1920.   (N. Lenin)